Partner with Angels

And Benefit Every Area of Your Life

channeled by Rae Chandran
with Robert Mason Pollock

Other books by Rae Chandran and Robert Mason Pollock:

DNA of the Spirit Vol. 1

DNA of the Spirit Vol. 2

Coming Soon:

The Dance of Hands

The Universal Codes of Creation

PARTNER WITH ANGELS

And Benefit Every Area of Your Life

channeled by Rae Chandran
with Robert Mason Pollock

LIGHT Technology PUBLISHING

For more information about special discounts for bulk purchases, please contact Light Technology Publishing Special Sales at 1-800-450-0985 or publishing@LightTechnology.net.

Also available as an ebook from your favorite ebook distributor

ISBN-13: 978-1-62233-034-8
Published and printed in the United States of America by:

Light Technology Publishing

PO Box 3540
Flagstaff, AZ 86003
1-800-450-0985 or 928-526-1345
www.LightTechnology.com

Table of Contents

Acknowledgments .... **ix**
Introduction .... **xi**
Information for Those Who Want to Know More xii
The Angelic Support System Awaits Your Call xiii
Angels Want to Help xiv
About the Angels xv
Call on Angels as Part of Your Routine xvi

CHAPTER ONE
The Benefits of Working with Angels **1**
The Importance of Angels 1
Call on Angels to Change your Everyday Life 2
Angels Are Available 3
Anchor Purity and Peace in Yourself and Your Community 6
Call Forth the People Who Will Make a Difference 7
There Are Angels for Everything 8
Embody the Energy of Michael's Sword 10
Use Michael's Sword to Sever Outmoded Beliefs 13
The Sword as an Instrument of Creation 15
Meditations to Anchor the Light of Faith 17
Call on Angels during Times of Need 20

CHAPTER TWO
Prepare for a New Consciousness **23**
Become a Universal Citizen 23
Connect with the Angelic Light City 26
Have the Courage to Accept a New Reality 27
Practical Applications of Energy 28
From a Caterpillar to a Butterfly 30
A Window of Opportunity Is Available 32
Reset and Fine-Tune Your Innate Natural Rhythm 33

CHAPTER THREE
Design Your Unique Path **37**
Your Specifically Designed Curriculum 38
Connect with the Energy of Numbers 39
Sacred Geometry Boosts Your Energy 40
Open to the Energy of Discernment 40
The Truth of Who You Are 41
Methods to Open New Energies in the Physical Body 43
Divine Dedication Starts with You 45
Make Angels a Part of Your Family 46
Remove Limitations from Your Eight Core Cells 46
Your Custom-Made Path to the Heart of the Creator 47
The Eight Core Cells of Your Conception 48
Hold the Light to Find Truth 51
Anchor Absolute Courage 53
Divine Your Future 56

CHAPTER FOUR
Access Support from Celestial Bodies **59**
Love and Support from Home 59
Connect with the Sun to Become One with Everything 61
Initiation with the Earth and the Sky 63
Call Forth the Seeds You've Planted in Other Lifetimes 65
Work with Planets and the Karmic Board 67
Schedule Meetings with the Karmic Board 68
Saturn Can Help You Through Hard Times 69
Create a Bridge to Other Realities 70
Kundalini 72
Rejuvenate Your Body with the Moon's Energy 73
Activate the Moon Chakra to Support the Emotional Body 75
Discover the Illusions of Your Soul 76

CHAPTER FIVE
Invoke Vibrational Support and Activation **79**
Miles to Go before You Sleep 79
Never Lose Hope 81
The Key to Your Next Life 82
Purify and Shift Your Vibration 83
Heal Vibrational Patterns 85
Changing Your Vibration Is Quicker Than Energy Work 86
Healers Can Call on Tahariel 88
How to Maintain the Vibration of Love 88

Open the Golden Heart and Activate the Torus 89
Experience the Buddha Within 92
Experience the Sound Vibration of Your Soul Name 93
Awaken the Adam Kadmon Energy Within 94
The Adam Kadmon Key 95
Ground Yourself with Dragon Energy and Dragon Codes 97

CHAPTER SIX
Practice Universal Communication 99
Learn to Decipher the Voice of Your Soul 99
Receive the Energy of Your Soul 100
Work with Color to Connect with the Soul 102
Alter the Energy of Business 103
The Sky Can Help You Remember Why You Are Here .. 107
Your Supporting Energies Are Waiting to Be Discovered109
Creative Inspiration 109
Imagination versus Inspiration 110
Preserve Wisdom and Intelligent Writing 112
Connect with the Wisdom within Mount Shasta 113
Activate Diplomacy for Effective Communication 114
Mediation for the Energy of Diplomacy 115

CHAPTER SEVEN
Develop Environmental Connections 119
Show Appreciation for All Creation 119
Water Is a Universal Connection 120
Connect with High-Vibrational Water 122
Align with Seasonal Frequencies for Balance 126
Cold Supports Awakening 127
Connect with the Four Seasons 128
Call on the Love of Flowers 129
Breathe Fully 130
Support Earth's Small Creatures 130
Send Your Energy via Flight 131
Ask the Universe 133

CHAPTER EIGHT
Revitalize Your Health and Well-Being 135
Energize Your Food with Its Original Consciousness 136
Celebrate as You Cook 138
Use Sound to Manifest, Heal, and Comfort 139
Access Your Unique Sound 142

Essential Oils Increase Vitality and Healing 144
Experiment to Identify a Smell That Supports You 145
Invite What You Want to Experience 147
Spiritual Alchemy Treats Common Ailments 148
Activate the Rainbow Code for Healing 150
The Rainbow Pyramid Technique 152
The Trial of Birth 153
Separation from Your Soul Group 154
God Danced the Day You Were Born 156
Water Birth Supports Our Transition 157

CHAPTER NINE
Rejuvenate Your Physical Body 159
Putting on the Hat of a Master 160
Make an Intention Book 162
Laughter Is Great Medicine 163
Request a Resurrection Ceremony 164
Insight from the Channel 165
Go into Your Next Life with a Higher Consciousness 166
Angels Can Replace Your Cells' Consciousness 167
Release the Energy of War from Land and People 168
Transition Angels Alleviate the Fear of Death 169
Experience the Power of the Resurrection Prayer 171

CHAPTER TEN
You Are the New Masters 173
The Beginning of an Era 173

About Rae Chandran 175
About Robert Mason Pollock 176

Acknowledgments

The "family" of participants in the Skype sessions lives in many parts of the world. Fredaricka and Mordechai are from Israel. Christine, Jan, and I live in Massachusetts. Rae and Cathy are from Japan.

Kryon's teachings through Lee Carroll have had a major impact on Rae's journey, and some of those teachings are paraphrased in this book.

Deonna Phillips pre-edited all the transcriptions and checked them against the recordings of the sessions. Christine read over the edited versions of the sessions and compared them to the original recordings for accuracy. Cathy proofed the manuscript, and Liz Stell formatted and proofed the manuscript document. Thank you all.

— Robert Mason Pollock

Introduction

Archangel Michael, Archangel Gabriel, and Archangel Metatron

This is Archangel Michael. Now is a time for new material and new teaching to be brought forth. Time is speeding up; things happen so quickly now. The speeding up of time corresponds directly with the speeding up of your evolution and your vibration. Look at your world. You see many things happening that were not happening last year; there is so much conflict in the news. To counteract this, you need new ideas and new teachings that can bring healing to people who are willing to listen.

Many people are stuck. They say, "This is my experience," and they want everything in life to relate to their own experiences. Many spiritual people say, "This is my truth." That is fine. It is their truth. But you must be open to what you do not know. Are you willing to open up and say, "There are things that I do not know"? Very few are willing to do this. Our teachings that come through Rae are for people who are ready for more. Soon you will see more new teachings to support the new level of awakening for people who say, "I want to know more."

The teachings about DNA and even this book would not have happened a few years ago. Many people cannot conceive of the ability to partner with angels. They would have called these teachings blasphemous. But those who are willing to listen and be open to them might find that these teachings can change their lives.

The problems on Earth are multiplying, and they cannot be resolved with old ways of thinking or acting. Solutions found with old thinking will only be temporary. The issues will perpetuate. You see this happening in Afghanistan and Iraq.

A new consciousness is needed for those who want new truth. Only with a new consciousness can you create a foundation that will sustain goodness. Others will follow. This is why we encouraged Rae to accept the assignment of channeling this book. With love, you must include heaven in what you create. In everyday life, most people believe that the work of their souls is for God, but everything else — their finances, their jobs, and their relationships — is theirs to do. When many people are presented with a new idea, they intellectualize it, finding logical reasons why the new idea will not work. That is the old way of thinking. Now everything should be combined and then created from that combination of energy.

Your support team is very powerful. In your own life, you must call forth your support team, even when your basement is filled with sewage. You can call people to fix the problem, but you can also ask your angelic support team and your guides to support you in resolving these situations.

Bring God into every moment. When you go to the supermarket, ask your guides to show you what you need to buy to enrich your life. Work with your guides and your soul every moment, for you are inspiring others to make this connection. You are building a new foundation for your life.

Information for Those Who Want to Know More

Rae lives in Japan, and Japan is prone to earthquakes. In the earthquake and tsunami of 2011, most of the damage happened to old buildings. Tokyo had little damage, especially to high-rise buildings. The Japanese developed technology to deal with the effects of earthquakes.

Something similar is now true for human beings. Use this new spiritual assistance, this new technology, to move with the challenges and never be overtaken by them. This must be done in every aspect of your life.

I loved what you said about asking for help with seemingly mundane issues like a computer that crashes or a basement that fills up with sewage. I could use help with those things.

You will be inspired. We will imprint you with our ideas and our thoughts if you ask us to support you. We will share our wisdom with you to create a new reality. The teachings in this book are for people who say, "I want more. I do not know, and I am willing to learn more." They are not for people who say, "This is it; I know it all."

There is a real thirst for new understanding about angels — how they can support humanity and their role in human consciousness. Many angels will speak in this book. Each has a specific vibration, a specific talent, and a specific purpose. Some will even give guidance about how to work with them in one area of your life. They are specialists. There are angels with specific tasks, and they are professionals in their own areas. They are ready to support humanity. They have already been supporting humanity.

There are many more angels than humanity knows. They will speak with one voice: "How can we support and empower our brothers and sisters, for this is our mission."

Blessings, this is Archangel Michael.

• • •

The Angelic Support System Awaits Your Call

This is Archangel Gabriel. Understanding angels can support humanity to move into a new consciousness in a much faster, smoother, and simpler way. Angels play a very large role in supporting humanity, but very little is understood about them. They play a much bigger role than any other support system available to humankind.

Once humans start accepting the role of angels, you will see a massive shift of consciousness, for angels have the capacity to shift consciousness en masse. As you are well aware, every human being has been gifted with angels to support them, especially after the year 2012. It is imperative that you start calling on them to change your life and to bring peace, security, and joy into your life.

Very little is understood about angels. You see paintings of angels in churches — a man with two big wings and sometimes a sword. That is all that people understand. Angels are the thread that holds creation together. Angels carry out the work of the Creator. They play such an important role that without them, humanity, Earth, and even other parts of the universe would not exist. This is why my brother, Archangel Michael, asked Rae and others to bring forth an understanding of the importance of angels in the new consciousness. Once their importance is understood and internalized, you can easily move onto the new road much more quickly and smoothly and in a joyous way.

The power of angels can shift any obstacle from your path. Angels are here for only one reason: to support human beings in the glorification of their souls. When you decide to say, "I am going to be on my path. I will walk my soul walk. I am going to call on the angels to support me in this," we will be there in an instant, for our desire is only for the glorification of all people who celebrate their souls.

You are probably aware of the books now coming out with different angels speaking. Angels are playing a much bigger role now. Just imagine if all people were able to hold the vision that angels are an important part of their lives. What could happen then, dear ones?

The consciousness of Earth would change.

Angels would be able to be seen.

Visually seen?

Yes. If collectively you called them forth, they would appear to you. This is the consciousness we wish for humanity to accept at this time. Collectively we can make huge changes. Call on us, and when you do, we will be there in an instant to show you the potential you have in your life to create a new reality. You see the example of Rae and others, whose lives have shifted dramatically after connecting with angels.

This is not just for one person. It is for everybody. Call on the angels, Robert, for your move to Greece, to learn the language, and to create the abundance that you need. Call on the angels to support you in moving the cats in the most benevolent way as well as in every other aspect of your life. People only call angels when they need them, like parking angels. What about all other aspects of their lives?

The purpose of bringing this material is to bring the awareness of angels in a much more practical, easy-to-understand way.

Blessings, this is Gabriel.

Thank you, thank you.

• • •

Angels Want to Help

This is Archangel Metatron. Did you know that all ascended masters are angels? You can see the contribution that ascended masters have made to the world. How were they able to accomplish this?

With the help of the angels, I would assume.

Exactly, because they were angels. They have left their mark on the world.

It is a privilege to be involved with this amazing work!

It is our privilege to work with you. It is always a cocreation. We are not able to bring forth anything into the world unless we have human help.

I hear you, but it wouldn't get far without you.

It is time to start accepting this role too, dear brother Robert — the grandness of you as you participate in building a new bridge between the human and angelic kingdoms. We are doing half, and you are doing half, so it is an equal partnership always. We cannot do anything for humans unless they ask for it, and it is done through human form.

Thank you, dear brother, and we will be with you, but as mentioned by Gabriel, call on the angels for moving to Greece the easy way, for your cats to move, the papers to come through, the financial situation in which you have enough money to go — everything. You can call on angels for every aspect of your support system. You do not have to know their names. Just call on angels for support: "I would like to get support for 'this situation,' 'that situation,' and so forth."

Okay, sounds good to me. It's a pretty daunting thing for me to move to Greece, but it is falling into place, and I know I will get help with it. Thank you.

Also, you can ask the angels to support you in finding like-minded people in Greece as well as good tenants when you move. They can support you in bringing you inspiration.

Thank you!

• • •

About the Angels

This is Archangel Michael. Very few people know about the angels speaking to you. There is now a window of opportunity for these beings to come through, so enjoy every one of them. Choose to work with the angels you feel some connection to through your heart. All of them will have individualized wisdom to share with you.

Are these angels you host working under your specific technology?

They work through the will of the Creator. I am presently in the position of holding the energy for all the angels who are speaking. I work directly with them. In common terms, you could say that I am the commander of all.

Along that same line, Archangel, I have a question. I am asking this in human terms based on my own experience in this lifetime: Were all of these angels created for the specific purposes that they now fulfill, or do angels move around into different positions?

These are angels created for certain purposes. But there are angels supporting beings on other planets and also angels supporting ETs. These angels were specifically created for the Earth plane.

What is the difference between an angel and an archangel? Is there promotion back and forth between the two realms?

We would not call it promotion, but like everything else in the universe, everything is vibrating and moving forward. This is why it is said that everyone is evolving. God is evolving. In the same way, angels are evolving. Archangels are evolving.

Is it possible for an angel to evolve into an archangel?

Of course, in the same way that you can become an avatar after going through many initiations and many lifetimes of work.

Call on Angels as Part of Your Routine

Each challenge you face during everyday life is an initiation to see whether you are able to maintain the light, even when you are persecuted or challenged. These are the tests in the days of grace. It is a test for you, how you are in relation to what is happening. If you allow it, you can control it; if you completely surrender to it, you can flow with it. There are many interacting energies. In ancient times, initiates constantly went through tests to move to the next level. But in the new consciousness, the tests are in everyday life. How you live everyday life despite what is happening in it determines whether you are ready for the next level.

We are eager to bring forth understanding because when you are able to work with angels, many of your problems can be shifted. This is because angels carry an intense energy of love known as cosmic fire energy. This energy can create a different reality by removing the obstacles or challenges in your life. Angels have been pouring this powerful cosmic light into the Earth plane, keeping Earth from tilting on its axis. It is the angels who have stabilized Earth's axis. If they can do that for the planet, imagine what they can do for you.

Many advanced cultures work with this energy constantly, calling forth the incredible power of the angelic realm. We wish to bring forth this understanding. Make us your partners. Consciously choose to work with us and also work with your mighty I Am presence. You will open a different reality. You may not even know our names. Intentionally ask to bring forth the sacred fire of the angels from the purity of your heart. You will see a difference in your life.

Many challenges facing humanity can be easily resolved with this incredibly powerful light. This is the understanding we wish to bring forth. We can be called forth by saying, "I call the immortal power of the angelic host. I call the eternal flame of the love of the Cosmic Christ, anchored by the angels, into me." Every day you can say, "I call on the law of the great angelic host with victorious mastery in the physical world." Or design your own words to say in everyday situations and endeavors. We can work instantly in any dimensional reality.

We have the capacity to change and instruct energies. For example, a teacher from America recently told Rae that in a previous life he was assigned to a rescue helicopter in the Vietnam War. When he was on a mission and under fire, he said he saw the incredible light of an angel coming and protecting his helicopter. There were 317 bullet holes in the helicopter, but no one died.

The message of this book is simple: Partner with us. This can only benefit you. We are real beings, and we can be called on to help in every area of your life, including your issues of abundance, health, business, and relationships. Consciously work with us. When you die, your loved ones who have passed away will be there. You will also see angels. They will be there ministering to you, helping you move into the next realm. It is the same when a child is born. When you enter the room where a child is being born, you feel the incredible love. You could say that the child is emitting a beautiful light. This is true. But when a child is born, the energy of angels is also in the room, supporting the mother and the newborn. You feel great love.

When a mother and a father hold the baby for the first time, they often say that they have never felt that kind of love. This is because the baby is fully infused with the love of angels. We are with you through birth and in death, whether you believe it or not. Many people believe they are imagining what they feel. Nonetheless, you have the truth.

Throughout this book, we will bring forth different angelic beings. Each holds a particular vibration or quality and is here for a specific task to support humanity. We will introduce them to you. You will learn about them and the ways they can help you. This book will help you develop a better understanding of the nature of angels and how they can support humanity.

CHAPTER ONE

The Benefits of Working with Angels

Archangel Michael, Angel of White, Michael's Sword, Angel Faith, and Angel Sharr

I am Archangel Michael. We bring forth understanding about the nature of angels and the support they can provide to humanity. We are happy that there are people who are receptive and willing to help us bring forth this understanding, for in this time of great change, angels can help tremendously.

The Importance of Angels

Angels will be able to shift the entire energy and create a new reality, the reality of time. They carry a much higher vibration than human beings are capable of because they do not come from a particular dimension. They are way beyond dimensions. Some people speak of six or seven dimensions. Certain teachers are from certain dimensions. One drop of angel energy can transform you. We want human beings to call on us for support.

Those who know about the life of Jesus and those who have read the book *Anna, Grandmother of Jesus* [by Claire Heartsong] understand that Jesus was part of a large family that lived in a community. The members of this community constantly communicated with angelic beings. From the time Jesus came to the planet, angels supported him. Angels brought the news of his birth to people. Throughout the book, there are references to angels and how they were able to support him. The energy for the healings done in the pool in Jerusalem passed through the power of angels, churning and energizing the water so that people could be healed.

Throughout history, Christianity and other religions include information about angels. They are called by different names depending on the culture. They always support humanity. Why do humans not work more with angels? So much has been written about them. You might say I am biased toward angels. Yes, I am biased, because I know these beings can truly lift humanity in the shortest time span. Many people work hard spiritually, and spiritual work can be measured in years, sometimes lifetimes. When you work with angels, you will see a difference in a matter of days. You will see more and more teachings coming from angelic beings, especially when the energies of polarization are very intense on the planet at this time. Knowing that angels and other support systems are available can instantly shift your reality.

Hospitals are surrounded by angels. When someone dies, angels are there. When someone is born, angels are there. When an execution takes place in a prison, angels are there to comfort the soul during its transition. Any time a person dies violently, angels are there instantly. Human beings cannot see them, so they are not aware.

Many children's stories are written about angels. One of the most famous angels is Tinker Bell. These stories convey deeper messages than what is read by the child. They were designed to open up the imagination. Angels are very real.

Call on Angels to Change Your Everyday Life

Human beings have very little understanding of angels. Angels can shift many things and bring changes to everyday life. If you call on them and ask them to pour their light into you, everyday life situations can be shifted.

You can call on angels to support you in any endeavor — situations in everyday life or on a planetary scale. You can communicate with them and change the energy structures. Like a wall that protects humanity, we often stand between you and destructive forces. The more you call on us and the more you love us, the more we will come to you.

Part of our work is holding energy in almost all places of healing — hospitals, nursing homes, and even prison medical wards. We have constructed light structures on our plane, and we pour our light into these places. The more you call on us, the stronger our connection becomes because when the receiver acknowledges the light, there is added value between the giver and the receiver. Call on angels to ask that your cosmic love of the angels (the cosmic fire) supports you in whatever you seek.

Your soul always seeks glorification and perfection. You assist this by manifesting what your soul chooses. What do souls seek ultimately? They seek the freedom to create. Ask us to support you in the creation of your soul's perfection.

In times of great change on Earth, angels have always appeared and held the light. During times of great inventions, when there were breakthroughs after breakthroughs to revolutionize humanity on a massive scale, we held the light so that new understandings could be accepted by the masses. Within times of great breakthroughs in medical sciences and engineering, we were there holding the light so that human beings could bring forth innovations that could change the world. During the time of the great illumination of the world that you call the light bulb, we were there.

In all moments of history when a breakthrough was imminent to support the shift of human consciousness, we were there. This is how powerful we are. Every time an ascended master works, we are there. Every ascended master is an angel, but not all angels are ascended masters.

Angels hold and pour forth love and the eternal flame into sacred temples, keeping the energy alive. Many inner temples where people go for healing and manifestation are kept alive by angelic presence. Call on them. If all the people in one state collectively called on angels for protection and guidance, that would call forth incredible energy. The angels would protect that state. We stand between you and any destructive force. This is why we are contributing to this book, to bring greater clarity and understanding about the roles angels play.

In the Middle East, various factions are warring. Will they achieve their intended purposes? Only people can decide that. If people call on us, we can be there to support those who are suffering because of this situation. Since our energy is of the utmost and finest vibration of love itself, it has the capacity to dissolve any dark energy.

We see so much ugliness in the world, and more ugliness is coming. What can the average person do during this time of great turmoil? You will hear and read much channeled material about how you must stay in your heart. That is rather difficult, is it not? You get sucked into current events and are often not able to hold what you know to be true. Call on us, and we will strengthen your resolve so that you can stand in peace, even in great turmoil.

We encourage you to work with angels. They will be the future teachers of humanity. There will be other teachers as well, but the understanding of angels has the potential to shift human conditioning and human thinking.

Angels Are Available 24/7

You will see that angels are not only of one denomination, such as Christians. Angels are found in all traditions, but they are called by different names. For example, in Nepal and Tibet, they call this energy dakini. They appear during moments of crisis. People see a light and say, "The dakini came to support me." They are we. In India, we are called devas. They are we. Even the grand religion of Islam talks about angels, how an angel appeared through the master. The Jews are well aware of the roles angels play.

Acknowledge the presence of angels in your life every day. Thank them, sending your appreciation and gratitude, and they will shower you with the incredible light of transformation.

You were saying that we can call on angels. But do they also appear without being called?

They do appear, but only in moments of crisis. Sometimes your guardian angel or healing angel appears. But when you consciously call them, with the purity of your heart, you will see their energy manifest in your life. Your life will become much easier.

So it is better to ask for help or ask for their presence?

Call for their presence; call for their help. You will see how things will move much more easily for you.

I have a hard time manifesting changes that I know I need to make. Can angels help me make these changes, or is that request too selfish?

No, of course that request is not too selfish. We said that angels can support you in your everyday life. If someone is ill, call on the angels. Ask them to channel their energies into you because, as you know, your soul seeks to glorify the God within you. We support this. This glorification is done by manifesting what you are seeking. Angels are not just for healing. They are a part of your everyday life. This is the understanding we want to bring to humanity. We are a support system available to you twenty-four hours a day. Call us forth, connect with us, and make us your friends by thanking us, appreciating us, and of course, most importantly, loving us.

Sometimes I face very difficult situations, and suddenly, I have an idea about how to do this thing. Do angels supply those ideas?

Your soul often brings forth solutions to a problem. Angels can also support you by bringing more choices, more understanding, and more clarity about how to get things done. But we might have a different perspective and a different understanding than your soul does. This is not to contradict but to support what is given to you by your soul.

My concept of angels has always been that they are just floating around, and it's not like we are supposed to call on them (in Christianity, anyway). They are just there to be merciful. The concept that you are presenting is that we can call on them constantly.

They are not just floating around. They have specific purposes and duties. They are in service to God and humanity to bring about change.

Yes, call on them often. Make them your best friends. Communicate with them and love them. They are here to support humanity completely. What better system is there than this? You always have them. They are always with you. Call on them when you wake up in the morning, during the afternoon, and before you go to sleep. Have a continuous conversation with them, and you will see how your life can change. Call on angels. They are the miracle authorities. Call on the miracle authority of the angels to be present in your reality to bring forth an understanding and a conclusion for what you seek. They can completely shift your reality. You might call this a miracle, if you so choose.

Entire cities can be transformed. Entire neighborhoods can be transformed. Crime rates can be reduced. Polarization can be reduced. Hatred can be reduced. Our love, our cosmic fire, is the antidote for all ills of society. Imagine the incredible power of angels and what they can do.

You must set aside what you have learned, and say, "I am ready to look at a new understanding." Your old understanding does not support you in your new reality, so be open to looking at a new reality.

There will be new interpretations of the Bible, the Quran, and the Bhagavad Gita in the future. The New Children will take up the task of bringing forth more true understanding. And that can shift a whole lot. They will see who God is and who angels are. They will see that the universe is teeming with a support system of millions, and humanity can call on this support system. The more you call, the more will be given and the more they will be in your presence.

Are the angels very specific in their duties? Are there many different categories of angels?

Millions and billions, each having a specific task.

I was trained in a meditation and contemplation format to call forth the beings of inner truth, inner reality, and other beings. Are they the same as angels, or are these a more specific energy?

Angels can bring clarity to what you ask. What you are truly asking for is guidance for your inner seeking. You are asking to open your soul to bring forth this understanding. There are many beings inside a human being. You are a group of consciousnesses. You ask the energy inside you to bring forth understanding of what you seek. With angels, you can request what you want to manifest, understand, clear, heal, transform, or transmit.

It is time to look at a new understanding of angels and God. You could say a combined energy of the Creator, a unified force of energy that contains everything.

• • •

I am the Angel of White. Archangel Michael graciously asked me to speak today. I have never spoken directly to humans before, so perhaps I will not be able to say much, or my sentences might not come through clearly. I am honored to be in your presence and to bring forth understanding in a new way.

Anchor Purity and Peace in Yourself and Your Community

You are all aware of the significance of the color white. White is called purity. In weddings, you wear white. In church, you wear white; the priest wears white. In many traditions, you wear white. But does white only signify purity? White also signifies peace. What is God? You will say God is love. Yes, that is one aspect. Another aspect is peace. What do you think?

The Hebrew language has a very beautiful word for peace — *shalom*. Call for me and ask me to anchor my energies into you. It is not only love that is awakened but also the peace of your soul, the peace of God within you.

The world is going through great turmoil not only because of war but also because of the fear of sickness, among other things. If humanity were to collectively call me, the Angel of White, we could anchor my energy together. What do you think would happen? We, the angels, are not allowed to do the work of humanity. But we can anchor the energy that you request so that you can work with energy to create a new reality. We need human bodies to carry out the work. You can anchor the energy of the Creator's peace by first inviting me permanently into your home and later into your community, your school systems, the prison systems, and the court systems, where judgment is made.

How can one human being judge another, even if he or she has committed a crime? You can ask me to anchor my energy of peace into hospitals, military barracks, and police stations. I am available to be called forth for the peace of God to be anchored anywhere.

The Lady of Liberty represents freedom in the grand land you call America. Can you imagine a peace statue, a peace stone, or a peace crystal? If you want to have peace in your life, work with us. Invite us in. There are no words to describe this peace. You experience it when you die, but why wait until death when you can have it now?

I encourage you to anchor my energy in your households. See for yourselves. When you experience my energy, you feel it and realize the truth of this vibration. You can work to anchor me in all the realities you choose. I am the Angel of White.

• • •

This is Archangel Michael. The Angel of White is grace itself. Call on her, for God is peace. God is love. They are two sides of the same coin. God is love and peace, peace and love.

Call Forth the People Who Will Make a Difference

In the journey of life through revelations and experiences, many people come into your being; some leave a mark, and some do not. Most do not. You can call on the people who will make a difference to your life and who will leave a mark on the planet. Here is a gift available to humanity.

You have the capability of calling people who can give you a deep and growing awareness of your life. Because of these people, your life will grow greatly. Some people come into your life and completely change you for the better. For example, Rae met Robert Shapiro and read his book [*The Explorer Race*, Light Technology Publishing, 1995] and also read the teachings of Lee Carroll. When you look back, you can see how your life has become enriched because certain people came into it.

In your meditation, you can call forth the people with whom you have not yet had contact. You can call for them, and say, "I am ready." You will see; these people will enrich your life deeply. We are offering this gift to humanity at this time.

Once the intention is made at that level, you will see many beings coming for this call, a gathering of your soul family. When this happens, your life is never the same again. Some members of your soul family might not stay very long, but they will definitely leave their marks. Some people can also leave a negative mark on your life. I am talking about the positive experiences, people who come into your life and enrich it. You feel blessed to meet these people. What a gift they are in your life!

This is a gift offered by spirit through the Karmic Board[1] and others. You will see. People will be attracted. They will hold similar aspirations, perhaps the same energy pattern, or they will work on themselves to create a better life or something similar. Nonetheless, they will make a positive contribution. We suggest you call these beings forth. They may be in other parts of the world, but distance does not matter. They might connect with you through telephone, Skype, or email. They will come, and it will create a beautiful experience.

As you look at your life, at the beautiful mosaic you have painted, you will see parts of the painting are by these people. If these parts were not there, your life would not have been the same rich experience. Many beings are not aware of this. This is directly tied to opening the not-known contracts. Many people are not aware that they have new contracts to be opened. They are content with their lives at the moment but are unaware that deeper aspects exist. There are new contracts to be opened, and these people may open them.

When we call our soul families forward, do we specify them by name?

No.

So you don't have to actually know who these people are?

No, of course not.

Now I think I understand this. It is not about people who have influenced you greatly in your past.

About 80 to 90 percent will not be from the past. They live in the present reality but not in *your* present or *your* reality. They are still here on the planet.

Understood. We have contracts with each other that have not been fulfilled at this point.

Exactly. This is one of the gifts we want you to open at this time.

There Are Angels for Everything

There is an angel called the Angel of Friendship. Some people cannot make friends. That is of their own making. This is like calling on the angel known as Angel Faith. When you work with Angel Faith and her energy, she can anchor and activate many energies directly connected to the faith inside you, changing the energetic patterns in your brain — your thought patterns about faith. It is

1. Rae Chandran, *DNA of the Spirit, Volume 1* (Flagstaff, AZ: Light Technology Publishing, 2014), p. 195.

similar to working with the Angel of Friendship. You can call on this angel to help you shift your mindset about friends so that you will be able to attract true friends in your life.

There is also an Angel of Harmony. There are millions and billions of angels. Did you know that there is an Angel of Digestion? There are angels for planets too. Angels protect each planet. The planets are spiritual forces.

There is the Angel of Leaves. Have you marveled at the intricate designs of each leaf? They are so beautiful and so well laid out, like the work of a master carpenter. Where did this beauty come from? When you look at all the different kinds of leaves, you see how they have been so beautifully designed. Angels bring forth weather changes too. Call on the fall angels, spring angels, winter angels, and summer angels.

We want to expand your mind to look at how angels are here to support humanity and how they work by placing certain thought patterns into people's minds. It triggers awakening and remembrance. This is the purpose of this book: to help you understand that angels are in every part of life. This realization itself can shift your consciousness, knowing that angels are everywhere. They are real, and you can communicate with them. When you acknowledge that angels exist, they will pour forth more of their energy, and they will become a part of your mind.

There is even an Angel of Tears and an Angel of the Heart. Call for these magnificent beings. There is an Angel of the Flower of Life. There are angels for every conceivable experience. You have heard people speak of the Angel of Death. It is a common term. But no one considers that there is an Angel of Birth. Birth and death are very similar. They are energy attunements. How about calling on the Angel of Operations when you face for surgery? Angels have built light centers above every hospital throughout the world. There is an Angel of Buildings, an Angel of Boats, and an Angel of Water.

We are opening your mind to the possibility that these beings are here in support of Creator. Their only intention is to support humanity to manifest like the Creator so that you can live joyously and peacefully and connect with who you truly are. This Archangel is Michael. Do you have any questions for me?

I am not in question mode. I am in receiving and listening and understanding mode. I don't have questions. My impression of this is that the world is a magical place, and there is so much support.

Exactly. This is the understanding we wish to bring forth. Earth is a place of immense beauty with support systems available for people who remember, understand, and know. This support system is available for every man, woman, and child on the planet.

But we need to ask.

Yes, but you cannot ask if you do not know.

Now people will know, so they will know to ask.

No, not everyone. Some will see this as imagination or fantasy.

Well, some people will ask.

Most people will.

Embody the Energy of Michael's Sword

It is a time for new beginnings. We wish to bring a subject that is very dear to me. It has been spoken of rarely. Please give me a moment.

• • •

Dear friends and family, I am the light of the sword of Archangel Michael. I have rarely spoken. It is time that the truth about me is understood. Rae requested in his prayers that I come forth to bring understanding, for this sword has always fascinated him. This sword is the truth, wisdom, and love of the Creator.

Like you, I exist on many dimensions. Archangel Michael uses me frequently. This is why you see me in his hands more than in any other angel's. I do not belong to Archangel Michael. I Am That I Am. I go where I am needed and called forth. I was created by the light of the Creator to support angels and all others who seek my assistance.

I can be as small as a pin or as large as this Earth and the universe. I encourage you to participate in gathering my energy. Embody this energy within you, and you can be a part of this sword, for this sword not only protects but also heals.

There are many realities in the universe. I can travel through all realities in an instant. You can use me as an instrument to safely travel to other dimensional realities, for there is nothing that can touch the sword. I hold the blazing light of the Creator. There are beings in other realities, but they do not have the same consciousness or intent as all of you do. They also know the sword is so powerful that they do not come near it.

You can anchor this sword in your home as a protective energy or call it

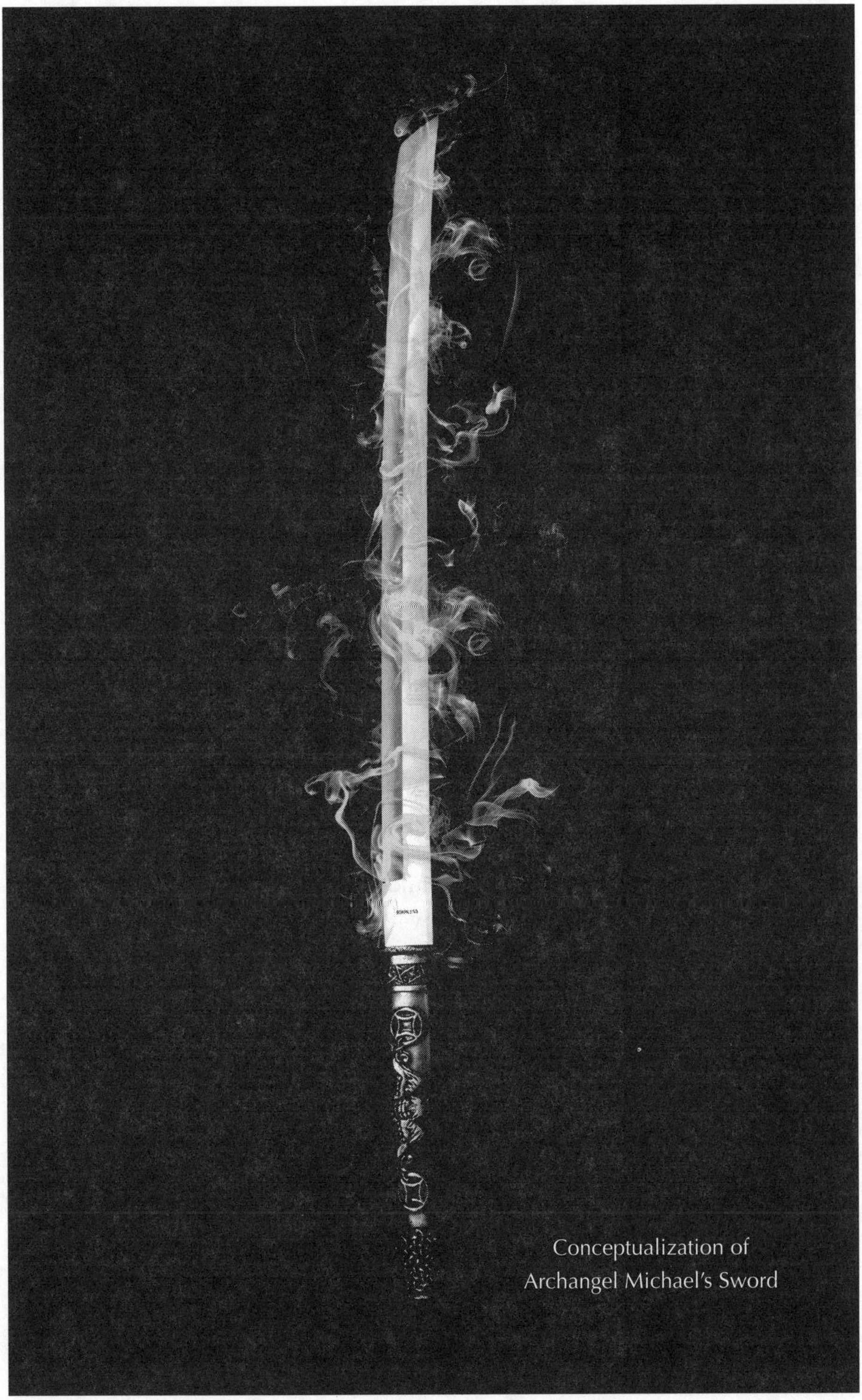

Conceptualization of
Archangel Michael's Sword

forth before you step out of your house. It is a shield of light that protects you as it surrounds you in its incredible beauty and power. Through intention, this sword can also be multiplied a number of times and in a number of realities. We encourage you to do this, for it can serve you and humanity, including when you work with nature.

You can ask that the sword be placed in your hands to bring forth the desired outcome by breaking through illusions. Imagine a beautiful, blazing sword in your hands. If you want to carry it, you must practice with it. It will become a part of you. Call for this during meditation, and feel the power surging through your hands, into your shoulders, and then into your belly, anchoring it there.

You can call forth this sword to pierce through your veils, your deeply embedded patterns, and the karmic energy that you are not aware of. My blazing power running through your chakra column will implode and explode so that what is underneath can come forth. You have seen the power of volcanic eruptions. Just imagine the power of a thousand volcanoes erupting inside your chakra column, bringing forth this incredible light within you. I am recognized as Michael's Sword throughout the universe by angels and other beings, including dragons and the spirits of mountains and rivers.

You can anchor me in polluted waters and ask that my blazing light cleanse and purify the water. Ask that the organisms that might have died be regenerated and new life forms be created in dead oceans and dead waters. Recently you saw a great hurricane in Japan.[2] People reported the perfect eye of the storm. You can ask me to pierce the eye to reduce the effect of a hurricane or a tsunami.

Angels often invoke their power flame, and we encourage you to use it as well. The angels who work with the power flame use me. When you call forth the power flame, the angels will anchor this energy into you. We encourage you to make this a part of your life.

You can ask that my blazing light be anchored in all buried souls, clearing the ground and releasing the embedded souls still stuck on the Earth plane. In the conflict in the holy land of Jerusalem, you can ask that we cleanse and purify the mosque at the Dome of the Rock[3] so that both peoples can come to pray in peace at this holy shrine. A time will come when both peoples will pray at the same place, and there will be harmony. A third temple will be built for both of them.

---

2. For information about the hurricane, go to http://www.usatoday.com/story/weather/2014/10/08/super-typhoon-vongfong-japan/16912813.
3. The Dome of the Rock is a shrine located on the Temple Mount in the Old City of Jerusalem. See http://en.wikipedia.org/wiki/Dome_of_the_Rock.

I am Michael's Sword. I hold you in honor, love, and dedication to the light. Blessings.

• • •

Use Michael's Sword to Sever Outmoded Beliefs

This is Archangel Michael. In the history of Earth, my sword has only spoken to two or three people. We are very honored to be able to bring forth this understanding, for you are ready. You have asked for it. This sword can be used as a vehicle to move to other realities safely and confidently, even to other dimensional realities.

I'm very humbled and grateful to hear these words and feel this power. It seems that the sword is a great source of healing for many aspects of Earth and her people.

It is a blazing sword of light. It was created not just for me but also for all of humanity. Many do not understand this, because you only see the sword in my hand, but as the sword said, it came from the heart of the Creator. It is a blazing light of truth, wisdom, and love. It is for all of humanity.

You mention working with the eye of a storm to help the outcome. How do we do that?

In your quiet time, ask the sword to be placed in your hands. When you feel the vibrational energy, ask for the support of your guides to transport you into the eye of the storm. Then pierce the eye with the sword of Archangel Michael until the eye disappears. You will see the effects happening as you look outside.

The fear of what is happening and of what people are watching on television compounds what is already there. If everyone would turn off their televisions and meditate on making the storm disappear or break down into smaller parts, then that would be the reality. But because they watch it on television, people become afraid. Fear is a very strong emotion that easily becomes reality.

Why do I work with the sword, and why do people see me with it? The sword is a powerful savior. Am I a powerful savior? I would say that you are all powerful saviors too. Saviors of what? Saviors of evil intentions in the mind. Evil is first created in the mind. I carry a sword of truth at all times. When you call on me to seek clarity in a situation — you want to see the truth in your personal lives or for something else — I will work with you directly. I will place my sword in your energetic body and cut through all illusions to show you the truth of the situation so that you can decide whether to choose a new reality.

People knew about angels in ancient times. We are mentioned many times in the Bible. Other lightbeings were known in India, but they were called by another name. Angels have been known throughout history as a representation of God's energy, supporting and protecting humanity. Human conditioning and thinking made angels in feminine form. There were also fallen angels — demons or Satan. No one has fallen.

In my case, people depict me as a strong male figure holding a sword, as a protector. They call me an angel of protection. There is some truth to that, but we are much more than what humans can conceive. We have a much larger role. My role is not just for the Earth plane but also for this universe. I work with Shiva and the Holy Spirit. It is through shattering something that a new consciousness or a new reality can be created.

You can call on me and ask me to release or shatter what has long been gone but is still connected to you energetically, whatever still has an influence over you. I will use my sword to cut these cords, especially of pain, guilt, shame, resentment, anger, and hatred. You might say, "I do not carry any of these." But if you look deep inside, you will see that you carry them at some level. Do you not carry anger? Do you not carry hatred? Do you not carry resentment? I am sure you carry them at the deepest level. You must be honest.

Ask me to dig deeper to bring them out and heal them with my sword of light. Ask that my sword release you from energies or entities from the past or from other realities (even with all your spiritual light). Ask that all karmic energy — from the past, from your ancestors, or from your land — that has served its purpose (but still lingers at some deep level) be cleared and purified. The same thing goes for star energies and star connections. They have served their purposes but still linger at some deep level. Just let these go.

The energy from the matrix [mass consciousness] is holding you down. People say, "I am a lightworker. I am not afraid of the matrix." I say they are still affected by the matrix in a big way. The collective system of thinking and beliefs is very strong. It affects us tremendously. That thread should be cut. We need to be aware of the collective consciousness.

There are also threads of wisdom and light. Keep them. All other things can be shattered, even the old belief systems about God and God's role in the universe and, most importantly, your relationship with the Creator within yourself and to the spirit of all creation. If you ask me to, I will sever all these cords. You have outgrown your need for them, but you still carry a part of that reality in many ways that you do not truly admit, understand, or realize.

My commitment to humanity and to the Creator is that if called forth, I will step up and support humanity in this. This is my promise to you and my promise to the Creator. This is what motivates the angelic realm and me. We are truly in support of and in love with humanity. Blessings. This is Archangel Michael.

• • •

Blessed beings of light, we are the angels who support the sword. There is a support system even for Archangel Michael. Our purpose is to support the sword, for it is not just a sword to cut through illusions. That is only one of its purposes.

The Sword as an Instrument of Creation

The sword also creates universes by transmitting light. The light goes from the sword with the intention to create, whether this is a geographical location, a planet, or a star system. It creates a specific form and then this form is saturated with energies from many beings. The sword creates the form to be filled with energies, where any kind of life form can exist. That is the true purpose of Archangel Michael's Sword. It is the greatest creator of forms.

When you connect with Michael's sword and ask that its light create a pathway for you to find the highest in yourself, the road will be open unto you. Are you ready for this road to be laid before you with the Sword of Archangel Michael?

It is through lightning and thunder that many countries and places are formed. The geographical shape of a country is formed through the sound of thunder and the flash of lightning. Ask that your soul be connected with Archangel Michael. You can ask to create your own island complete with paths to walk using the sword. It will be tailor-made for you. Since it is tailor-made, it will be of the purest vibrations and essences.

One must have a pure vibration to step into this, for what will fill this new road, this new geographical location or island for your own path? There are many colors emanating through the sword — metallic blue, bright red, turquoise, pink, white, and green. Ask for the colors emanating from the sword to be anchored into your being, and see the roots of the blue lotus awaken within your back. There are many roots, and each root has a specific color emanating from the sword. When this happens, you will remember your individual path designed by Archangel Michael's Sword.

Make the sword a part of you. Carry it consciously with you throughout your day and throughout your night. The light from the sword is anchored deep in your hips, through your mind's eye. Your blue lotus is fully awakened and fully glowing all the time. True magic begins to happen.

We are the angels who support the universal sword of Archangel Michael. We are called Ahram (*AAhram Wa Ni*).

I have a special connection with the Sword of Michael because that symbol has shown up for me many times in many ways. I really feel myself clothed in this beautiful blue light. I feel as if I now have my traveling clothes.

You are in a very expansive state, and next year you will see many expansive ideas coming into you. Have courage to experiment. Work with the many new thought forms coming into you and with this sword to create new pathways to walk on your own island (your own road), and you will create magic and miracles.

I would like to ask what the blue lotus represents.

Adam Kadmon.[4] You are a blue being. Do you know that? All of you are blue beings.

Is creating your own island and your own path simply having the certainty of mind over matter?

4. In the Kabala, Adam Kadmon is referred to as the original man. See http://en.wikipedia.org/wiki/Adam_Kadmon.

This is not mind over matter. It is an opening in your heart and a knowingness. This is a path, and this is an individual design for you by the sword that created this entire universe now creating an entire universe for you. If you look at the story from your own Kabala, all masters had their own individual paths of finding God and ascending. This is what we are saying. Someone designs an individual path through intent and requests.

• • •

Meditations to Anchor the Light of Faith

Hello, dear family, this is Angel Faith. What does "faith" truly mean? There are many interpretations. From our perspective, it is simple: Believe in yourself completely — not in a foolish way by viewing yourself through rose-colored glasses, but by believing in your immense divinity and sacredness. Great masters who walked the planet have this kind of consciousness. They believed. They remembered. We ask all of you to have this kind of belief — belief in your sacredness — every day.

Place your hand over your heart, and say, "I believe in my own sacredness, in my own divinity, for I am a divine soul having a physical manifestation." This will start the process of activating the energies of faith within you, for there are specific glands in your body that can support in opening the consciousness of belief. There are also certain flowers, flower essences, and plants that can support you to have more belief, faith, and trust in yourself. Look for these essences and flowers. There is potential for you to have more belief and faith in yourself.

The Creator, in his benevolence, has provided support in your third-dimensional world. It is easy to forget who you are. You can also call on me, and I will anchor the light of faith. Ask me to light the candle of faith within you.

Right now, close your eyes, and bring your attention into your solar plexus. See a beautiful golden candle in your solar plexus, in your mind's eye. It could be small; it could be large — a beautiful candle.

See the light of this candle emanating its energy into your being. Your full attention is on this golden candle, for there are glands and tissues in your physical body that support the activation of faith in yourself. These glands and tissues are situated in your hip area, especially in the back of the body. See this light from the candle slowly moving into your hips. They are completely filled with this golden light.

From the back of the hips, the golden light seeps through the back of your feet, all the way to your ankles and into the soles of your feet, especially all your toes. There is great energy there, the energy of regeneration. Your hips all the way to the toes are filled with the beautiful golden light coming from the candle. Breathe in and out three times.

You can ask me to place a mantle of energy (like a winter cloak) called faith around your shoulders. See the energy from this cloak going into the back of your body. Every human being once had great faith, but because of past karmic energy, most have lost faith in themselves and in all other aspects of life, including God. This has come about mainly from experiences of times as cave dwellers, and these energies are still held in the back of the body. Have you ever wondered why you do some of the things you do? Where did this come from — certain habits or thoughts returning again and again? They usually come from past experiences, not from this lifetime or 100 lifetimes ago, perhaps 40,000 lifetimes ago.

The energy from the cloak will release many karmic imprints, things in your personal reality, especially in regard to having trust and faith in yourself. When you have trust and faith in yourself, you will also recognize that you are a sacred, divine being. You realize that you are God, indeed, in physical form.

You will see some movements in your back, and the blue lotus will be activated along with the torus energy. We ask you to hold this vision for a moment in the back of your body. The blue lotus has some other components to it, for its roots are golden and fully anchored in your hips. A beautiful light will start emanating from this blue lotus into the back of your body, going all the way up your back to your neck, activating your soul essence chakra and returning, and then moving again up your back to the back of your head and to the center of your head. This energy is anchored in the middle of your head.

Give the intention that this blue lotus will always stay open from now on, emanating this light of belief, trust, and faith in your own sacredness and divinity. This cloak will always be there unless we remove it. Work with it for the next few days. It will become part of your present reality. You may open your eyes, dear ones, at this time.

You mentioned 40,000 lifetimes. Did you really mean 40,000 lifetimes or 40,000 years?

Forty thousand lifetimes.

Really?

How old do you think you are?

Not that old, but I guess I need to revise my beliefs!

I would say almost 100,000 years.

Where is the soul essence chakra?

It is in the back of the neck. It is a very important place. It is an eleven-point star with a beautiful soft-purple light emanating from it.

I feel like I want to close my eyes and rest. I feel as if I've just been bathed in a beautiful, hypnotic energy.

Actually, once the activation of the blue lotus is done and we are able to anchor it, it becomes a part of you. You will be in an immense expansive state. So even if you have problems, you are much bigger than the problem, and you are able to hold your peace. Your communications and responses come from this immense peace. When you are in this space of peace, you can also activate the twelve pillars of light within you containing the total essence of God. You are in a very high state of awareness at that moment.

I feel the imprint of this experience within me, and I feel this has been the missing link to my self-worth, to really embrace the divinity of my soul. I really thank you for this.

Now, Christine, we ask you to do another experiment. Are you ready? We are going to challenge you.

When you are in a quiet space, light a candle, or have a candle, some flowers, or a glass of water. It does not matter. Sit in a chair, and in front of you, have a small desk. Put another chair there. Invite your mother to come forward. Communicate to your mother from a place of love. She will have many things to say to you. Do not be judgmental. Allow this to happen. You will be able to hear from her perspective. When that happens, there will be a lot of healing. You will see why she did what she did. Then what happens? Completion.

There will only be love for her from you. When you heal yourself, you are healing your past and your future too. Then you will appreciate and say thank you for the gift that she gave you. Are you ready for this?

Yes, I am very ready for this.

• • •

I would like to ask about which flowers and plants strengthen faith.

This is a very important question. It is our secret, but we can say this particular flower is beige in color, and the plant name starts with a *W*.

Angel Faith says goodbye to all of you. She is available for consultation and companionship with all sisters and brothers of light. This is Archangel Michael. Let us say thank you, Angel Faith.

Thank you, Angel Faith.

• • •

Call on Angels during Times of Need

Hello, dear friends, my name is Sharr. I am the angel who works with humpback whales and some species of dolphins. These creatures are very dear to human beings. They are truly sacred beings and possess vast amounts of wisdom and knowledge, including the history of this planet, its purpose, and why it is in the Milky Way.

Dolphins and whales make sound frequencies, tones, and harmonics. These sounds are misunderstood and misrepresented by the scientific community. They are for communication, but the true purpose of these beings is to support DNA. You can call on humpback whales and ask them to download your own frequency of sound tones into you. It might be only one word — such as *ah*, *uh*, *wah*, *wuu*, or *yah*. When your frequency is downloaded and you tone this sound, your cellular structure awakens to its fullest. Whatever has been embedded in your cells (from your belief systems, thought patterns, behavior in past lives, and ancestors or cultural heritage) will fall away. This sound can help you remove the plaque — the embedded energy in your cells that is not of light.

These sounds can be very simple, *mmhh*. It could be as simple as that. Ask that your specific sound vibration be anchored into you. You can do it at night. These beings are here to support humanity.

Most children around the world clap their hands and shout when they see whales coming up for a breath. Most adults try to take their picture. It is time for humanity to understand them and their purpose here.

Pink dolphins are rare but are still seen in some places. They were present during the great deluge that damaged the planet many years ago. My purpose is to support humanity during times of natural crises. A natural crisis reawakens old memories of survival. Humans have been deluged by natural disasters and also by predators.

Great terror happens subconsciously with a feeling of utter helplessness. Hopelessness can set in, and people can give up completely. They might even want to die.

Dolphins appear during times of natural disasters, perhaps one or two or a pod. By sending love, they affect the subconscious and unconscious minds of humans: "This too shall pass, and you will be all right. You may have lost many things, but you still have your life, and if you choose, you can dream once again."

We support human beings so that they do not fall into utter depression or complete helplessness. We can also assist you in your personal lives, and we will anchor these energies into you if you call on us. When hopelessness sets in and you have no energy to move forward, you lose your enthusiasm for life and wait to find peace at the end of your life. This is a false truth.

Call on us, and we will anchor the energy of not being completely helpless and hopeless. There are situations in the Middle East and Africa in which people are giving up hope. Each of you has the capacity to call on us, and we will provide the energy where it is needed. One person can do it. A hundred people can do it. The effect is the same.

Blessings. We are the Angels of the Humpback Whales and Dolphins.

CHAPTER TWO

Prepare for a New Consciousness

Archangel Michael, Light City Angels, Angel Uvayah, Archangel Jeremiel, Archangel Metatron, and Angel Ezriel

This is Archangel Michael. I want to give you one word. It is a powerful word. One of the challenges you face is how to connect with your soul and how to connect with your higher self.

Close your eyes. Breathe three times, and repeat this word as you focus on your third eye: "Ellio." Keep focusing on your third eye.

How do you feel?

Speaker 1: Very focused.
Speaker 2: I feel a strong connection with my feet; they are grounded.
Speaker 3: I feel my third eye opening up.
Speaker 4: I feel the focus.

When you do this, you will feel an expansion. When you do this regularly, you will feel your I Am presence coming into you in a matter of minutes, communicating with you. "Ellio" is a simple word. We ask you to practice this to see whether it can support you.

We feel that connecting with the I Am presence has been a challenge for many people. Many lightworkers say, "I have been doing everything, but now I am truly able to connect with my I Am presence."

• • •

Become a Universal Citizen

Hello, family. We are the Light City Angels, supporting the feminine — the feminine goddess and all feminine beings, including human beings and all who create the feminine. There are millions and billions of us, supporting all forms of humanity, for the feminine creates.

There are feminine and masculine trees. Some mountains and lakes are feminine. You can feel the difference when you say its name. The same is true with waterfalls. Some waterfalls are very masculine and some are very gentle and feminine. This is not understood at this time. There are feminine flowers and masculine flowers. There are masculine vegetables and feminine vegetables, masculine shapes and feminine shapes, and masculine home structures and feminine home structures. We support the feminine.

You are ready to experience the light city. The light city is supported by the feminine. One of the most predominant feminine figures supporting Earth's transition is Mary Magdalene, and there are many others. When you ask to be taken to the light city, the feminine beings who support planet Earth (along with us) will help you. Connect with the light city beings, light city plants, and light city buildings. The entire city is built by light, and you can integrate the light from the light city by interacting with everything in it.

The beauty of the light city is that it is created by you, for you. It is a reflection of you. When you are in the light city, imagine and visualize many beings of light, brilliant colors, brilliant light, and brilliant vibration, as high as you can go. They reflect the light that you have given to produce it. You will see a quickening of your light vibration, and your feminine aspect will be further opened and brought forth.

You can call on the goddesses who support the light city and on us to integrate the light from the light city to open you more fully to your feminine aspects. You will move into the place of creation, for the light city is a place of creating with the Creator. This is a gift we offered to Rae recently, and we now offer it to all of you. We are the angels who support the feminine energy on this planet.

• • •

Do these angels represent the female energy soul of the messianic energy that is coming soon?

This is Archangel Michael. They are preparing for the next several months. They will be sending much more energy here to prepare for the new consciousness, which was born in April 2015, through which you can move more fully into your true soul purpose and create from there.

Is the hallmark of the new consciousness unification with the soul?

A big shift is happening, yes.

Are the light city and the etheric temples one and the same?

From our perspective, they are different. The light city is created by you, for you to be in cocreation with the Creator, using and bringing forward the feminine part of you.

Would you say that these light cities we are building around us are extensions of our auric energy?

They are formed from the energy of your I Am presence as you start cocreating with the Creator. You are going to start creating much more fluidly, and much more easily, from a place of knowingness. You will create the highest benevolence — what is good for you and for others — using the feminine aspect of yourself, which births new creation.

The feminine energy will settle into every heart from the light city. Every experience you create will come from your feminine aspect, which is the loving aspect of creation. Of course, you create now, but when you start creating from your feminine, you will come from a place of higher vibration. This is how great masters are created. When you create from the feminine, it touches a much larger energy field.

We wish to bring forth the understanding that from now on, human beings can create using the quantum electromagnetic field energy of Earth and the entire galaxy. You will be connecting with the Seven Sisters of the Pleiades, and your creation and your thinking will shift to a much higher level. You will start seeing less of yourself and more of us. You will still have your family and your loved ones, but you will also start seeing us. You will be part of a much bigger picture than you had conceived. You will become a world citizen — a universal citizen.

When you create from the perspective of a universal citizen, what you create is much more magnificent and comes from a much higher perspective. Also, when you start connecting with the energy of the light city, you will energize your body. Giving will become more important, and you will give your energy freely. You will not be depleted, because the feminine naturally gives.

Go to the light city. Create your light city in the grandest vision you can imagine, and see the beings there you saw from the time of your creation. This is the next level for all of you — to move into this place of creation. When you intend to create from this place, manifestation happens much faster and with a higher perspective, using the energies from the galactic plane and eventually the Pleiades.

We are bringing forth concepts for you to experiment with and experience. These can shift your personal reality. You must believe that you are much bigger than you think you are, and you are moving into a new reality. You must hold this thought and believe you are worthy of this.

If you believe you are not worthy, then you cannot create anything. You *are* worthy of this gift we are offering you. You all have raised your vibration to be able to receive this. We do not offer this to everybody. But we want you to put this in the book so that once people know such things exist, they can work to attain the level to create their own light cities.

Connect with the Angelic Light City

Do we create our own light cities, or do we go to one that already exists within us?

It is both.

We would become as interconnected stars, much like a web going all over Earth to lift the spirits of many people. It seems like colossal changes could happen.

Of course, when this happens, you are protected. You would not be affected by situations like the Ebola virus. These lower levels of vibration would not even come near you because you would be blazing with light.

In some ways, are these light cities similar to DNA in that they are already there? All we have to do is activate them? Is that true?

Yes, exactly. When you activate them, you will also start connecting with other light cities created by great beings of light, including ascended masters. Why not connect with the angels' light city? Angels go there for nourishment. Angels have very difficult jobs. They send incredible amounts of light and love to the Earth plane, and they become depleted because of Earth's dense energy. They go to their light cities to be nourished and uplifted. Who maintains and heads the light cities all over this universe? I do, Archangel Michael.

In your meditation, you can say, "I give intention to connect with my own light city and that it be connected with the angelic light city." Also, you can ask that your light city be connected with a master you work with. The light city you have created will start vibrating at a much higher level. And your light city does not disintegrate when you leave your physical body. It is your creation in the hologram, and it remains there.

• • •

Have the Courage to Accept a New Reality

Hello, my dear family. My name is Uvayah. My task is to support the integration of life. What does the integration of life mean? Suppose you are in a deep meditative state and great light was anchored into your energetic field. What is the next step? There must be a process in which the energy that was downloaded is fully integrated into all your bodies so that it can have practical applications in your life. This is where many lightworkers have faltered. Energies are downloaded into their consciousness, but they are never fully anchored into places where they can be of use. Otherwise, the lives of those lightworkers would be very easy.

You are working with high-vibrational energies. Why are these not applied practically to solve everyday life problems? This is where I come in. I support the integration of the higher-vibrational energy downloaded into you by distributing this energy throughout all your bodies, organs, and physical realities so that they become an application you can use.

If you download an application to your mobile phone, it just sits there until it is fully activated. When you activate it, use it, and come to know it, it becomes useful to you; otherwise, it just stays there. This is similar. Higher-vibrational downloads into your consciousness can just stay there. They are not distributed throughout all your bodies. Call on me. Let every energy gathered during your meditations — or when you are walking, sitting, or going to a holy place — be anchored into your entirety. I will support you.

This is how great masters were able to do magic and miracles. They were able to utilize the higher light coming into them. Suppose you attend a spiritual workshop. You feel good. There is a group energy. You feel good about the material you learned. But can this be used to support your life? It must be distributed throughout your bodies. You are your own house. There is electricity coming into your house, but if it is not distributed throughout the house, only one room will have light. The others will stay dark.

Similarly, you may feel good now, but other areas of your life are not enlightened and have challenges. You are not able to utilize higher energy because it has not been fully integrated into your entirety, especially into your tissues, muscles, bloodstream, and skin — all your cells.

I invite you to request my presence after a deep meditation. Come into my ashram. We have a specific chair where you can sit. This chair is designed to anchor whatever you have gained in meditation into every part of your body. You will remember this energy, this upliftment, to change your mind, to get out of depression, and to be open to divine creativity, or any other form of higher expression of your deep meditation. Let me surprise you, dear ones. Uvayah is one of my names. This is Metatron. Blessings.

Practical Applications of Energy

Many beings are able to access higher energy, but how can this higher energy be applied as a practical tool in their lives? We are not seeing this happen. They feel good in their meditations. They get energy. They go to a workshop; they read a book. They find good information. They feel good and uplifted. But then what? Our interest and desire is that energy from higher levels — your guides, higher self, teachers, angels, or anyone else — be used to benevolently benefit you. You must be able to use this energy practically in your life.

We are with you all the time. Perhaps you are looking for someone with whom you can share your life. You have been meditating with this intention. How can you use the energy you have gained for this specific purpose? This is where I come in. I will distribute this energy appropriately into all parts of your physical body, starting from your tissues and muscles, and also into your auric body and other bodies. This energy will become the intention of what you want to manifest throughout your being, not just through your mind. Call on me. We will work together.

Every morning I connect with my oversoul. I set intentions, I align my energy, and I do a few other things. Is that energy then distributed throughout every part of my body? I feel fantastic when I connect with my I Am presence. Should I call on you then?

Do you feel it distributed to every part of your body? Are you able to support your life with this energy to create a new reality?

No, I don't know how to do that.

This is what I am trying to explain — how to use this higher-vibrational energy to create benevolent outcomes in your life, for what you seek, so that your life becomes much easier. I am not talking about you alone. I am talking about all humanity. This is so life becomes easier for humans. There will be more peace and joy in their lives. True freedom comes when you are able to create a life that you like.

This is what we are trying to say to people: "Yes you are all accessing very high vibrations, but how can you utilize this energy to manifest a new reality?" We have seen that many are not able to do this. This is what we wish to assist you with.

You said that you were bringing integration not just to the mind but also to the body. In other words, it went through one great synapse and then through the nervous system?

Exactly. To your muscles, tissues, bloodstream, and the hairs of your skin — everything. Your entirety carries this energy, and when you are able to make a decision or an intention from this level, it is often manifested right away because it comes from your entirety. This is how great teachers do miracles and magic. When a master does magic, what does he do? He uses his entirety to bring forth a desired outcome through one thought, one intention, or one prayer. It happens right away because it comes from his fullness.

The fullness, or the unity. The whole is equal to more than the sum of its parts.

Exactly. We are bringing forth understanding that is relevant to the present reality. We feel it is appropriate that people be able to open up to this new reality because people are ready for this new truth. We have never brought this information into the world before.

You are positioned under Archangel Metatron's technology?

I am Archangel Metatron.

Are you an aspect of Metatron?

Like you, I wear many, many hats.

Do you wear the hat of Shiva as well?

We are all part of one. The people of India may not know anything about Metatron, but they will easily be able to relate to Shiva.

This has never been taught before. This is very powerful. Why now? Why not earlier in our evolution?

Because everything can only be brought forth when it is appropriately timed to be received. Otherwise, it would not be accepted. People are now ready to receive and accept it. You will see many new things that have never been brought forth because people were not ready. Even this concept will not be accepted by some, but we know that you are ready to accept it, and the readers of this book will accept it. Still, there will be some who will say no. They have been carrying the same beliefs and are not going to change.

From a Caterpillar to a Butterfly

We want to paraphrase a humorous story from our precious brother, the Magnetic Master Kryon. There was a big, fuzzy caterpillar.[1] He was the king of the caterpillars, and all the caterpillars listened to him, for he was a wise ruler. What do caterpillars do? Munch, munch, munch, eat, eat, eat. One day, he gathered his followers, and said, "I heard a rumor that there is a new gift for caterpillars. Go into a box and be in a dark space for forty days and you will come out with flying colors — with wings! It looks suspicious. Do not eat for forty days and stay in a dark space? This is not good. Who is spreading this rumor? He may be the evil one, tricking us into forty days of darkness." So he beat his chest and called to the forest spirit. He asked about the rumor of going into forty days of darkness.

The forest spirit explained the new consciousness, the new reality, "Yes, it's true. This is the process of metamorphosis."

"Why didn't the big spirit tell it to us directly?" asked the caterpillar.

"Things have changed. We are each messengers for the Creator."

"Can you imagine not eating for forty days? This is terrible."

Then the forest spirit gently told him, "Look up, and see the beautiful butterflies flying in the sunshine, enjoying themselves."

The caterpillar said, "You are an evil one because you know we can only look down. We can never look up."

---

1. Lee Carroll, *The Parables of Kryon* (Carlsbad, California: Hay House Books, 2001).

The forest spirit said, "Why don't you just crawl on a rock, and then you'll be able to see further?"

"Oh, that is dangerous because there is no food on the rocks. You know we have to eat, always munch, munch, munch, munch."

The forest spirit said, "The seasons have changed now, and if you do this, you will become a butterfly. You will be able to escape the new season of rains and floods."

The caterpillar said, "You look very suspicious."

The forest spirit said, "Thank you, blessed one," and he disappeared.

The caterpillar went back to his followers and said, "I met with the evil one, and he told me that we must go into forty days of darkness and not eat, and then we will come out as butterflies. I know it's not true, so I dismissed it."

His followers said, "Hooray, hooray, hooray! You saved us."

The rains came and the ones who followed the spirit's advice went to upper branches and after forty days, became beautiful butterflies. Those who did not were washed away.

I am saying the same thing. It takes courage to accept a new reality. You will not only be able to maintain higher energy but also utilize it in your daily life. When your daily life is settled, peaceful, and joyous, then your mind is in a much better place to receive higher truths. This is the key. This is what we are trying

to bring people to understand. You must have at least some semblance of peace in your life. Otherwise, you cannot focus on spirit within yourself. This is what we are trying to achieve.

• • •

A Window of Opportunity Is Available

Blessed ones, my name is Jeremiel. Some also call me Jeremiah. That is a name given to me by human beings. I am one of the angels who came when Master Jesus was about to be born. I was one of the messengers who appeared to the shepherds.

What gift do I bring to my brothers and sisters of light for the awakening of humanity? You can call on me and ask for the energy of an enlightened mind so that a new consciousness can be birthed into you. I will clear the way. I will clear the cobwebs and other outmoded energies throughout your being so that a new consciousness can be born. You are coming to another important time in the history of this planet, the holy month of December. Every month is holy, but for many hundreds of years, people have been honoring this month as special. It has acquired its own connotations, and it has become part of the holographic image of the planet Earth. When you look at your own life and the lives of other people, you will see that December is much gentler. People are more giving, more open, and more forgiving.

December is a special month. There is a window of opportunity between December 18 and December 22. A very special window opens, and if you are clear, a new outpouring of consciousness can come to you and become a part of you. For that to happen, something needs to be prepared. Before you can move into the house, you have to construct the house. Before this new consciousness can be downloaded, call on me to clear the way.

There is potential during this time for a new star to burst forth onto the Earth plane. Downloading the energy from this star can bring forth a new way of looking at things, a new consciousness for the planet, a new way of looking at religion, and a new understanding of God.

I, Jeremiel, will support you if you call on me and not just during this time. You can call on me any time. If you want something to be cleared before you begin your meditation, call on me.

You are trying to access high-vibrational energy now. I will clear out and make space for this new consciousness to come into you so that it is not muddled with an old thought form or mental energy. It can be as pristine and pure as it needs to be. You can call on me tomorrow morning when you wake up, and say, "I call Archangel Jeremiel for a new consciousness, a new beginning to be opened unto me, to make space for any high-vibrational energy that might come or that I can experience today through this opening." You will feel much expansion.

For the sake of the record, did you identify yourself as an archangel?

Yes.

• • •

Reset and Fine-Tune Your Innate Natural Rhythm

This is Archangel Metatron. Remember always that you are sacred beings. Make every moment count, and you will raise your vibration. When you wake up in the morning, say, "I intend to experience this day as a holy day and create experiences that are holy in nature, for I am holy. So I will see the holiness in every person I interact with today or who comes into my energy field."

This simple statement made in the early morning will start the ball rolling. The more you remember this, the more you will raise your vibration.

• • •

My dear brothers and sisters, my name is Ezriel. I am the angel of rhythm. Life goes in rhythmic circles. There is rhythm in the universe. Everything has rhythm. The seasons come and go in rhythmic cycles. Months come and go. Time is in rhythm. More importantly, your body is in rhythm. It has a sleep cycle, a waking cycle, and a growing cycle. There is rhythm in the body that regulates all these things — a rhythm of the bowel movements, rhythm of the heart.

Eighteen other angels and I work with rhythmic cycles not only in human beings but also for all of creation on the Earth plane. We are responsible for all the beings on the Earth plane.

When you look at your life, you will see times of great growth and times of stillness. You may wonder what happened. There are bursts of growth that suddenly slow down. But nature does not work like this. Nature works in perfect rhythm. It is very rare for rhythms to change in nature. At certain times of the year, a tree will grow. At other times, the leaves will fall. It never changes.

Changes within the human body depend on a variety of factors. I can work with you to fine-tune your rhythmic cycles and set them permanently so that you are in the full rhythm of your body. Your body was designed to be in rhythm. But through abuses of your thought patterns, habits, food, culture, and the baggage you have acquired from others, you have completely lost the understanding of rhythm.

Babies are born with perfect rhythm, but the conditions in which they are born, the way they are raised (the eating cycles, foods, sleep cycles, what they see, and their interaction with their parents) disturb their rhythms. It has often been said that if you can once again become your natural self, you will restore the perfect rhythm with which you came into the world. Your normal self is something you have cultivated; your natural self is who you really are, your inner core self.

Call on me to reset your rhythm. The rhythm of almost all people is off balance, some more than others. All of you could use my help in resetting your rhythms so that your bodies can resume their natural cycles. When you are in your natural cycle, you flow with the universe. When there is a block in your rhythm, you suddenly run out of ideas. Your creativity stops. You do not know what to do. Blocks start when your normal rhythm is not in tune with your natural rhythm.

Look how effortlessly nature moves. Being in harmony with your natural rhythm will become critical in the coming months, for the planet is moving into a new rhythm and a new consciousness. You should be in harmony with the rhythm of the planet. Heaven moves in a particular rhythm. Earth moves in a particular rhythm. The elements move in particular rhythms. Everything that grows, other than human beings, moves in perfect rhythm.

Think about this, and if you feel it is appropriate, ask me to work with you (along with others) to reset your rhythm so that you can once again be in harmony with all.

When should we ask to reset our rhythms?

Right now. It is a good time to prepare. You are surrounded by rhythmic patterns — seawater, the fermentation of milk. Everything has a rhythmic cycle, and nothing is off-key except human beings. You did not know such things existed. There is very little attention paid to rhythm. We will work with you.

When we are meditating and we think of rhythmic bodies like the ocean, things that have a pulse or are rhythmic, can that also help us become more rhythmic?

Of course. You are taking it to a much higher level. You can tune in and give intention to experience the rhythmic pattern of the great whales. When they dive, when they come out of the water to breathe, and when they call their sounds, you feel a different energy. You will be in tune with them because they communicate with Mother Earth. They are helpers of Mother Earth. They give notice to Mother Earth about what needs to be done. You will be able to tap into that understanding.

I am Ezriel, Angel of Rhythms.

• • •

This is Archangel Michael. We hope you enjoyed the rhythms. It is very important to remember rhythm in the coming times. Rhythms will become more prominent in the world. Rhythm is an important part of healing.

When you are healing someone, think about rhythm for your clients and how they can be in harmony with the rhythm of the universe and Earth. Then they can have true, permanent healing. They will flow much more easily. They will be able to let go of things. They will be more accepting. Their minds will become clearer.

CHAPTER THREE

Design Your Unique Path

Archangel Michael, Angel Dina, Archangel Chamuel, Archangel Metatron, Archangel Maroni, the Angelic Beings, Angel Erelim, and Angel Eisiti

This is Archangel Michael. It is another lovely evening to gather and reawaken the energy of love and joyful companionship. During these times, the veil is parted, and we communicate directly with your hearts — and you to us. Indeed, it is a precious, cherished time for us all. Many beings surround you and listen to this in awe; however, only one of us speaks at a time. It is not only you who are touched by this special time. Many other beings are uplifted, empowered, and supported by this work.

This is a time that is cocreated by us in partnership. When you look at life, you see that everything is a partnership. You have a partnership with your children. You have a partnership with your spouse. You have partnerships with your family members and with your colleagues in the office. You have partnerships with your animal friends and your plant friends. You can strengthen these partnerships.

What does "partnership" truly mean? A partnership is two or more people coming together in support to create a specific outcome. In 2015, the year of 8 [2 + 0 + 1 + 5 = 8], you can strengthen and cement this partnership, and like all partnerships, if nurtured, it will blossom and enrich the lives of everyone involved. Make an intention, a conscious choice, that you will strengthen this partnership first within yourself — with your body, with your mind, and with your spirit — which will strengthen all the other partnerships you have, especially the one benevolent and loving partnership.

For example, Brother Robert has a partnership with the beings you call cats and with the beings you call wild birds, whom he feeds in the morning. Watch these partnerships blossom. Mordechai, you have a partnership with the

Holy Land. You have a partnership with ancient wisdom of the House of David [Davidic line]. Cathy, you have a partnership with the land. And Christine, you have a partnership with the supporting energies of healing and transformation. For all four of you, the year 2015 will be an expansive year in more ways than you can imagine. If you were to take note of what is happening now and again one year from now, you will see how much you will have accomplished, how much you have moved fully into your soul's purpose.

Now I would like to invite a new angel to talk about the importance of partnership and how it can be nurtured and supported. Here is a beautiful angel.

• • •

Your Specifically Designed Curriculum

Hello, my family. My name is Dina, the Angel of Wisdom. You might ask, "What about all the other angels, do they not have wisdom?" Yes, of course they have wisdom and love, but each angel has a very specific quality or essence through which it supports humanity on the Earth plane. I support bringing forth understanding from the universe and distilling it for practical application so that it can be applied on the Earth plane.

You can find much wisdom. Take any book, any material you read — there is much wisdom and truth in them, but there is very little about how to apply the wisdom and truth practically in your life. This is very important. You need to have a curriculum specifically designed for you.

Let us say that you are an advanced student at a university, and the professor designs a curriculum for you. He designs something very specific for you because he sees certain qualities in you, and he wants you to develop them further. By doing so, you will attain much more than other students taking the normal course.

My responsibility is to bring forth wisdom and distill it for individualized, practical application. How do I do this? Through using engrams, because I not only download this information but also make an imprint of the wisdom — using sacred geometric patterns — into your brain, solar plexus, hands, and legs. I call this "wisdom for practical living." You may also call this "walking wisdom" in which you are able to experience wisdom throughout every aspect of your life.

Call on me, and I will make this engram in specific codes for your reality. For example, Christine is a healer and a massage therapist. She wants depth of understanding about her methods and how they can heal on a much higher level. Work with me, and I will download sacred geometric patterns into your hands, which will strengthen their energetic vibrations for healing. The specific vibration I anchor will be different for each healer. This will be tailor-made for you.

Connect with the Energy of Numbers

There are specific vibrations in numbers. You know about this through numerology — 0 through 9. Meditate on these numbers. You will be able to feel their different vibrations. For example, connect with the energy of 0. Connect with the energy of 1. Connect with the full essence of the number 2. Do this with all the numbers up to 9. Why up to 9? There are nine patterns that affect humans in their manifestation of a desired reality.

Archangel Maroni speaks later about eight core cells that hold all the limitations you brought forth and stay with you throughout your life [see pp. 46–49]. Anchor the energies of eight numbers, from 0 to 7, into your eight core cells. Anchor the number 8 in the middle of your head and 9 to the soles of your feet.

You will see an energy shifting in your core cells. Some of the limitations of your belief systems will start falling away. You will start seeing things in a new way, just by the vibration of these numbers.

At least 75 percent of the energy in your eight core cells is not from this lifetime. You brought this with you. By using these numbers, you will be able to bring healing. When you start working with these numbers and heal your core cells, your work will affect your mother's life and her mother's life and her mother's life.

I have a question about a word you used that I am not familiar with — "engram." I have never heard that word.

It is an energy imprint that never goes away. When you call on me, I will make an imprint in your energetic field, your brain, and other parts of the body with the exact application of the wisdom that you need to create a specific and desired outcome. When you work with these numbers, we are able to remove many of the limiting beliefs, energies, and emotions you carry in your eight core cells. They set the limitations for your life. How many lightworkers experience an imbalance in some part of their lives?

These limitations that you are speaking of, are these from our own personal karma, or do they also involve family consciousness?

They originate in your mother's womb, and that means you are greatly affected by family karma. Family karma determines how you will be in this lifetime within small parameters of change (through your free will) after you start growing up. The earlier part of your life is completely influenced by your family.

What I do is custom designed for you. I am like a professor who has a special student and custom designs a curriculum so that the student can accelerate much faster.

Sacred Geometry Boosts Your Energy

How does sacred geometry transmit the custom energies?

Sacred geometry is divine geometry. You have geometric patterns in your body. The geometry resonates with the geometry inside you. It is like taking medication. You already have an immune system, but it is weak. A dose of medicine can strengthen your immune system. The sacred geometry boosts your energy. It works in partnership with the energy you already have. It complements and strengthens what is inside you.

I wonder how general that is. Was that just for Christine, or is it for anybody who is doing healing?

It is for all of you, but the energy to be anchored into Christine will be a little bit different from what would come for you. My work is to bring forth custom-designed, practical wisdom for each person. We honor you and thank you for this opportunity to speak with you.

• • •

Open to the Energy of Discernment

Blessed brothers and sisters, this is Archangel Michael. As you move further along in your own growth, you will be exposed to many new ideas, new information, and new knowledge. You must have discernment. With more growth, there is more responsibility.

Ask for the energy of discernment to be opened within you, for there might be times when you can be led astray. This does not mean that you should not look for or accept new ideas. You must judge to see whether this new truth supports you in the path you have chosen.

An incident happened to Rae in 2009 when he was in Egypt with friends. They went to the mountain behind the great temple of Hatshepsut. They climbed this mountain in the early morning because they had read that a French archaeologist reported extraterrestrial beings had built something there. They wanted to explore.

Rae and his friends climbed the mountain. They felt that they were very close, but they could not see any markings. They had to use their intuitive guidance to find this place. Then they saw an old man sitting, with a donkey nearby. He was selling water. They asked him whether he knew this place, and he said he did. They bought drinks from him, and he said, "Come with me. I will show you." Instead of following their own guidance, they followed the man. After an hour of walking, he took them to his house where he had some stolen antiquities. He was trying to find a buyer.

The lesson for Rae and his friends was that they did not trust their inner guidance at the last moment. They trusted someone who literally appeared out of the blue, and they lost the opportunity of finding what they were looking for. They were within 100 meters of what they were looking for. They could have found very good energy in that place. They would have communicated with the ancient past, but their minds came into play. You must ask whether whatever appears in your path supports you in finding yourself or your truth.

The Truth of Who You Are

An angel named Chamuel will speak now. His name means "one who seeks God." All humans seek God in their own way by doing things they think they need to do to find something. Humans sometimes feel the need to find something higher, but they often do not achieve it. Chamuel can assist you in knowing truth. You can call on this great being to help you completely focus on finding the Divine within you.

* * *

This is Chamuel. Each angel has certain qualities, and I would say, certain tasks (if you were to call them tasks, seeing that there are no tasks or certain duties under the guidance of Archangel Michael). My specialty is bringing people an understanding of God, how you can devote yourself completely. People often are sidetracked by this or that. When you call on me, I can guide you to be completely focused, for my name is One Who Seeks God. If you call me with all your being while in meditation, I will infuse you with my energy so that you can seek the God within.

I pour my light into humanity's mind every night during your sleep so that you can remember your true purpose for being born here. There are only two purposes for each person to be born — the glorification of oneself and the honoring of oneself through this glorification.

I work on you during the nighttime. Your mind is less chatty while you sleep, so there is a better possibility that you are able to listen. Beams of light from my heart can infuse light particles in your heart so that you can awaken and see this grand truth — to look at your life and understand that whatever you do is to glorify the Divine within you. We come from a very high place, so the angelic realms will support you in these efforts. If you call on me, I will place my hand on you and send a thunderbolt of light into your being.

Many energies within the human being are trying to express themselves because whatever is created always seeks self-expression. [Chamuel uses the terms "energies" and "beings" interchangeably here.] But many of these energies inside you seeking self-expression are not from the highest realm and do not carry the highest vibration. So when I send my thunderbolt of light into your being, many of the energies that are not of the light can be flushed out.

You must remember, all human beings are made up of many beings of light. Through the power of your thinking, actions, and beliefs, you feed these beings. Through negative thinking, these beings can become very powerful. And since they seek to express themselves, this expression becomes a reality. Thus, you forget why you are here.

You live in a world that you think is advanced, but there is very little spiritual understanding and a low quotient of light. Yes, technology has evolved, but your technology has not evolved to include spirituality. When you become addicted to technology through any means, you feed the beings inside of you. This is not of light. I do not want to use the word "competition," but I will just say that these beings inside you are always trying to manifest. So I (and other beings) pour energy into you so that light becomes more a part of you, and other beings without light can be pushed out.

There are energies right under your kneecaps. This is why the first layer we focus on in the DNA activation ceremony[1] is this part of the body. There is very significant energy there that can be tapped into and opened. The truth of who you are is not only in your heart but also in other parts of your body, including under your kneecaps.

Understanding the human body is important, particularly at this time, so that you can understand where the focuses of energy are stored. You can rediscover the ingenious way you were created and where the divinity is hidden within you.

---

1. Rae Chandran with Robert Mason Pollack, *DNA of the Spirit, Volume 1* (Flagstaff, Arizona: Light Technology Publishing, 2014) p. 317.

I encourage you to call on me when you have any misconceptions about the way you are going or when you feel that you are doing everything you can but are still not achieving what you want. Being able to connect with you so that you can feel and experience, I will be able to lead you back to the truth of who you are. That is the vibration I hold — true devotion. I worked with Master Sananda on this subject. He is the master of the sixth ray.

There are also energies in the back of your neck between your shoulder blades. If this energy can be opened, then once again you will know the truth of why you were born and the importance of the light within you.

True devotion is the act of being dedicated to yourself and glorifying the essence in you. People say they are dedicated to their spiritual practices, which might be true. But if you look deep inside and are very, very honest — utterly and brutally honest — you will see how small this is. Are you dedicated to this truth 24/7 or only when it is convenient for you?

Call on me to anchor the energy of true devotion. Also call on me to activate and awaken the energies that are still time coded inside your body so that you come to realize, once and for all, that you can be dedicated fully to the God within you. Devotion is not self-aggrandizement but a true knowing of yourself, experiencing yourself, and evolving yourself.

Methods to Open New Energies in the Physical Body

I am very grateful for the information you have brought forth. It is true. It is not easy, even if we want it to be, to dedicate ourselves completely and totally. The question is in knowing how to do that.

This is why I asked you to call on me, and I will work with you to open the energies that are still inherent inside, like a time-coded machine. You must open and activate these energies within you so that you can return to this dedication to yourself once again. For example, there are energies underneath your kneecaps and at the back of your neck. Also, notice that when your elbow hits something small, it gives you an electrical shock inside.

The funny bone.

Why is this so? Have you ever wondered why there is such a strong electrical current there and only there? This is a very strong force.

Close your eyes. Cup both elbows in the palms of your hands. Bend or fork your tongue in your mouth a little bit. Close your eyes and bend your tongue while holding your elbows. Give intention and imagine that you are breathing through your ears, sending the energy into your hands and to your elbows. You can even add a color to it, any color you choose. You are etherically creating a sacred geometric pattern when you do this. Let the energy flow through your hands to your elbows with the colors and your breath. You may remove your hands from your elbows and release your tongue now.

Where do you feel the energy? Did you feel anything?

Speaker 1: I feel my right hand pulsing on my left elbow.
Speaker 2: I feel my hands pulsing, and I also feel my heart beating.
Speaker 3: I feel the circular energy flowing through my arms and into my heart. It is also very pink.

Yes. These are some of the energies that have never been opened. This is why I asked you to call on me. I can guide you during your sleep to bring forth understanding of how you can open up more energy.

Here is another example: *Close your eyes and hold the tip of your nose with your thumb and index finger. Focus your attention on your toes. Breathe through the soles of your feet. Where do you feel the energy, dear ones?*

It feels like a tuning fork.

You will feel energy in the back of the body.

Oh, I see. Okay. Thank you.

What about you, Brother Robert?

I am beginning to tune into the back now and feel that.

Exactly. This simple exercise is done for two minutes. You will feel a lot of energy in the back of the body.

Is this at all related to the torus energy[2] in the back?

It is related to the energy of the membranes and true dedication to yourself. Yes, when you do this, the torus energy and other energies are definitely affected.

We ask you to realize your body is an energy machine from head to toe. Many other energies are not awakened at all. They are kept like future news, but now, with the new timeline, the planet has shifted, and you have shifted. It is time to awaken and open this. Even the word "ascension" you have, what does that truly mean? It means awakening to the full force within you. All these energies are

2. The torus is a donut-shaped energy vortex that is a recurring pattern in nature. To learn more, see http://www.thrivemovement.com/the_code-fundamental_pattern.

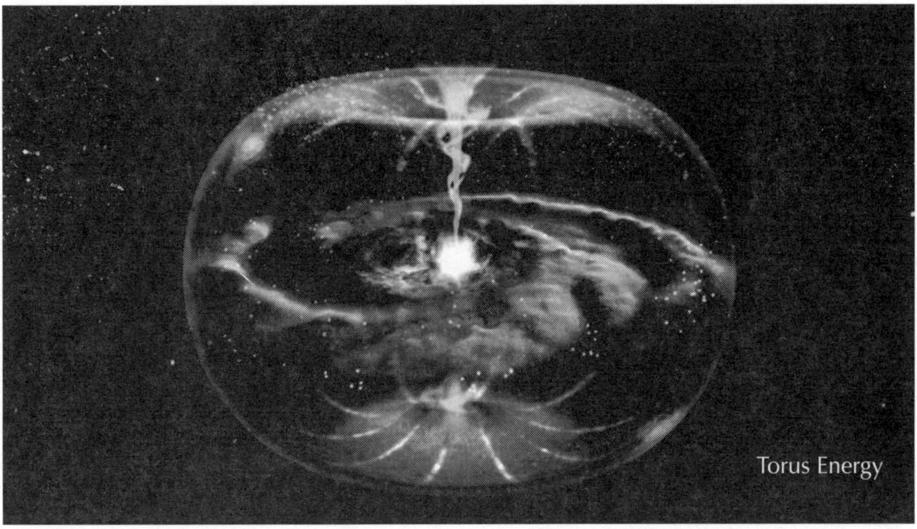

time coded. They are only released when you are ready. We, the angelic realm, can release the light in your body, mind, and soul so that it can be available to you again.

Make this intention today: "From this moment onward in my life, everything I do is to glorify the great God within me." When you make a statement such as this, we in the angelic realms will support you completely. This is Chamuel.

• • •

Divine Dedication Starts with You

This is Archangel Michael. We wish to bring understanding of some of the roles that angels play. We feel it is important to have clear understanding of what true devotion means. This is why I asked Chamuel to speak with you — so that you can understand and incorporate this quality within you. This is a very important aspect.

If you look at some of the initiations from the ancient past, from Egypt for example, the final tests were about devotion. To whom are you dedicated? Initiates were tested again and again to come to this place. To whom are you dedicated? To whom are you attached? We feel that this understanding of the One truly brings you back to yourself and to complete dedication to yourself. This is the foundation of your faith — your belief in yourself and in God. We just want to lay a foundation.

Call on Chamuel daily for the next three to seven days. He will strengthen you with this energy. You may think that you are dedicated, but it is always good to know that your energy can be upgraded. It is like channeling. People have been channeling for a long time. You must constantly update the vibration of your channeling so that higher truth and higher vibrational energy can come. You can say, "I am dedicated to my soul." Yes, but there is a higher vibration to that.

The same is true for creating with writing. There can always be a higher vibration with creative writing. Ask for higher vibrations dedicated to your soul be brought forth and incorporated into you at this time with the help of Angel Chamuel. You will give this gift back to yourself.

You must always remember that you are evolving every moment. Truth is evolving. Make it a habit to call for higher-dedicational energy every day or every month because your devotion to yourself will become stronger, and you will grow. This is Archangel Michael.

Make Angels a Part of Your Family

This is Archangel Michael. Work with the messages that are given to you if you feel resonance in your heart and if they support you, for we are in support of humanity. We have been here for millions of years, and we are still here. We are truly your helpers. Why not use the helpers? We sometimes act as coaches, sometimes as guideposts.

Call on us frequently. Make this a part of your life. Invite the angels you work with to stay in your heart. If you have room in your home, you can even put a chair there specifically for the angels. This chair is for this angel. It is called an angel chair. Make angels a part of your family. What do you do when you are living with your family? When you wake up, you say, "Good morning! How are you today? Did you have a good sleep?" It is the same when you wake up with angels: "Hello, my angels. Thank you for guiding and supporting me during my sleep." Make this a part of your life. When food comes to the table, you could ask, "Angels, how about energizing this food before I eat it?"

Incorporate angelic energy into everything. When you go out, call on them to guide and protect you, to open the cosmic fire within you. Call on the angels to support you with any personal problems. The more you communicate, the more they will be there. Invite them to stay at your house. Make them your best friends, your invisible light force. They will surround you, and you will find your life going much more smoothly. We are dedicated to human beings.

• • •

Remove Limitations from Your Eight Core Cells

Hello, blessed ones. This is Archangel Maroni. I rarely speak with the beings from this planet, but the great Archangel Michael has requested me today. It is my honor to be with you to bring forth some level of understanding.

I inspired the great faith known as the Latter-day Saints. I appeared to Joseph Smith[3] many times, downloading imprints, templates, and other instructions in a very clear, understandable way so that this new teaching could be brought forth.

Now, what can I do for humans of the present day? If you call on me, I will anchor a specific template relating to you and the Creator. Each human being's relation to the Creator is unique. The fingers of a hand all look alike, but they have different functions and manage to work in harmony.

In the same way, your connection to the Creator is unique. Ask me to download, or anchor, a template containing the understanding of your own direct connection with the Creator, how you can fully merge with the divine within you, and the great Creator from whom everything came.

We brought teachings to the Mormons because we felt that Christianity was not being adhered to in its letter and spirit. There was great distortion of truth as well as misunderstanding about the nature of reality and the nature of God itself. We felt that this particular individual I was coming through [Joseph Smith] had the potential to create a new reality for many, for he was a teacher in ancient times. He knew how to make the teachings into a structure and lead people. This is why we came to him, for it was part of his great plan. Over many lifetimes, he had requested that he be available to bring forth this new understanding. Now you can call on me to anchor the template of your direct step to God.

Your Custom-Made Path to the Heart of the Creator

All of you have been exposed to many realities of truth. Some of you have tried different approaches and have taken whatever you feel is appropriate or resonates in your heart. Other things you leave. This has all been very good. But I can give you a custom-made energetic blueprint for you to be fully within your divine soul and with the Creator. There are templates for each human held in the ethers of the Earth plane, as there are in the other star systems and other galaxies. There are templates for the beings living there. You are not aware that these templates exist in the ethers or how to bring this connection into your consciousness.

Each teacher is able to access, understand, or perceive a small aspect of the templates, and so much awakening has happened. If you look at human history, although humans have slowly awakened during the past few hundred years to

3. Joseph Smith founded the Church of the Latter-day Saints (the Mormon Church) in 1830. To learn more, visit http://www.josephsmith.net/?lang=eng.

come to the present level, it is still a primitive level. Nevertheless, there has been a progression. Why were people not able to attain the liberation that they sought? Why were they not able to grow as fast as they thought they would?

Look at the masters who achieved the grandest of missions — ascension. None of them followed the same path. They were shown their own unique ways of finding their paths during their quiet times. Sometimes this was downloaded into their entire beings during their sleep. You can find your individual path to attaining liberation only through observation. You will never attain liberation by following the path of someone else.

It will become critical for high-level students of mastership to be aware of this and say, "I am ready to climb my own individual steps, custom-made for me, into the heart of the Creator." Each human being is unique. Each human being has a different vibration. It makes only perfect sense that one path is not for everyone.

Your guides (Archangel Michael, and other beings of light) work with you, but have you ever wondered or asked them to show you your individual path? Perhaps not. You must now find that path. In finding that path, you will grow in your uniqueness — in your individuality — in your creation of experiences to find God.

There are energetic patterns in your physical body — in your lung area, behind your ears, and in your navel area — which contain vibrations or energetic imprints that lead you to your individual path. But you must ask for this path to be opened and shown to you.

If you look at fairy tales and children's stories, most of the heroes who conquered and won the princess' heart walked alone. They had help along the way, but they took their own paths. They created individual paths. I wish to download the new imprint of a custom-made path for each and every one who calls on me. Does this mean that you will disconnect from your other guides? I would say not. You will work in union with them, for they are waiting for you to make this choice. Then you will see an acceleration and expansion of your spiritual growth.

The Eight Core Cells of Your Conception

There is an energy called the center of life in the human body. The center of life is connected to the Flower of Life (or middle point) that exists in every human being. The center of life is a key element, for it contains the full essence of you. We are not talking about DNA. We are going way beyond DNA. You must activate the energy of your center of life. The center of life energy exists between the thymus and the back, below your neck.

It is important to unlock the center of life energy because (as you know) when conception takes place, cells divide. They divide many times — two to four, to eight, and again in multiples. The eight core cells that were created during conception remain with you throughout your life. The patterns of your life are in these eight cells. This explains why people who have achieved high vibrations are still not able to change at the deepest level. The energy in these eight core cells restricts the creation of a new reality. These cells remain with you throughout your life, and they are very powerful.

Many beings of high light fall down and do things that are completely incongruous. What happened? The energy of their eight core cells is so strong it can even override their high levels of vibration unless they are able to maintain it constantly. The key to changing your life completely is changing the energetic imprints of these eight core cells. All the limitations you feel, your belief systems, your faith, and your energy are in these eight core cells.

When you are able to activate the energy of the center of life and impregnate these eight core cells with your life energy, you will start to see a shift. You will be able to break away from many belief systems — your rules about yourself. Then you will see your unique path.

We ask you to meditate on the center of life energy within you and on these eight core cells. Ask, "What do I hold in my eight core cells that prevents me from having complete freedom and peace in my life?" True freedom is when you are able to create what you want. From my perspective and understanding, unless you are able to change the energy of these eight core cells, nothing major happens, or it would take much longer to achieve what you are trying to achieve. The choice is yours.

Would you tell us where the thymus is? I'm a little confused. I thought it was near the heart somewhere.

Just above the heart on the left-hand side.

You mentioned conceiving and multiplying. Was this the reasoning for polygamy among the Mormons?

We are not talking about that. We are talking about the core cells in the physical body when you are born. We do not condone polygamy. We were talking about the cells multiplying within a human body. We disapprove of polygamy. This practice is not in the interest of the highest.

We are talking about the multiplication of cells. When you were born, your cells multiply. During the multiplication, your eight core cells were also being formed, and they remain with you throughout your life. They contain all your limitations and your belief systems. This is very different from the energy of your chakras. Unless we fully change the energy of these eight core cells, nothing major will happen. Even if something happens, it will take a long time to manifest.

You are explaining the division of eight core cells, meaning two to the third power — two to four to eight — right? This is the essence and the source of everything that happens during a lifetime.

Exactly. This is why I have been asked to come at this time. You are in the year of 8 (2015 [2 + 0 + 1 + 5 = 8]). This is directly correlated with these eight core cells and what they hold.

Is there a direct correlation with the eight spheres in the tree of life?

Exactly.

So the one and the eight couple into an ionic bond. Am I close?

Dear one, very close. Yes. This is why it is such an important aspect to be revealed at this time.

I believe I understand that your service is to help us illuminate the eight core cells so that we can ask for patterns that have been improperly developed within us to be released. Is that true?

These eight core cells contain all the limitations you have brought into this lifetime. They must be replaced. When you start a spiritual practice with high-vibrational energy, some of your consciousness remains at the core level within the limitations of what you brought in from other lifetimes. True change can happen when we completely erase all the energies within the eight core cells so that we can infuse them with a new custom-built template for your own path.

This is why it is so important to have individual ascension paths.

Exactly — and also have the ability to create in your own unique way. Once you remove the limitations of these eight core cells, then you will start shining. You will understand that at your core, you are an amazing individual with a direct connection to God in your individual way.

Why has this information not been given before?

Everything has divine timing. When you work within your own belief system [or religious tradition], you will see major, massive changes in your life. Then I can work with you to bring your own path to you — your own route to God. It is very difficult to write a book about ascension or create a common understanding because the path to God is individualistic. It is not a collective path.

That is why ascended masters have walked alone.

Alone most of the time, almost everyone. They had help from many people, but in the end, they walked alone.

Yes, the higher you go, the more lonely the path.

It is an individual path, and others cannot follow it. Others must understand that this is your path.

It was truly a pleasure to communicate with all of you. Twenty fifteen is the year of 8, an important year in terms of completion and truly finding who you are and your own individual path. Blessings, this is Archangel Maroni.

• • •

Hold the Light to Find Truth

This is Archangel Michael with Metatron and a host of other angelic beings embracing you with the deepest and purest love vibration of the angelic kingdom. It has been a roller coaster year for many of you — for the entire world — but if you look back, you have come through unscathed, most of you at least.

You have grown so much. Even with all the chaos in the world, you are still able to not be swept away. This is a new you. This will be the normal you in the future. All around you will be chaos, but you will be at the center point, holding your light, continuing your work, and building a strong road. We thank you for this.

It is not easy when you see so much chaos outside, but you are doing well. Once again, we say thank you. Lightworkers like you will make a difference on the planet. There has always been fear in the world, and now the fear has accelerated. It is both manufactured and natural. Be aware that much of what is in the news is filled with distortion and untruth.

We ask you now to open up to the sacred parts inside you that carry discretion. You will see more fear-based news. In 2014, there was an Ebola scare. What has happened? Do you hear much about Ebola? Nothing. News coverage is down about 95 percent. Next it was North Korea hacking Sony's computers. Do not buy into what the government says. It is not North Korea that did this. Look for disgruntled employees of Sony itself. What better way to take the heat off an internal investigation when you can blame someone else? What can the government do in this situation? They will try to tighten the Internet rules and regulations so that they can monitor everybody. There is always a truth behind the truth.

We ask you to hold this truth, for many people will buy into the stories, adding power to the energy of fear. Ask that the energies of discernment and discretion be opened to you from your soul so that you can become aware of what is happening and be able to see the truth behind the truth, and then shine your light.

There is much evil in the world. On a higher scale, there is no evil. There is no good. But in a three-dimensional world, you must master the opposites, so there is evil on Earth. You can confront this evil by finding the truth and holding the light. Bring the light of compassion to all the people of North Korea, where the citizens are suffering, and to all nations where people still have pure hearts.

You will see more diversion tactics happening next year, mainly by your government, as well as others. During these times, they try to introduce legislation to suppress the freedom in people's hearts.

You may wonder why Archangel Michael is speaking to you today about this situation. It is because you are lightworkers. You need to open up to the discretion within you to see the larger picture in every situation.

Archangel, in this world full of lies, is it possible that all the governments will unite and pursue the truth?

It is our hope that one day all governments will come together and work to create abundance. This effort will be from more than governments. It will initially happen through businesses. They will make this great shift, bringing all people together. Businesses have agendas — primarily to make more money. But through that, there will also be a shift in politics. It is our hope that politicians can come together for the benefit of humanity. It is a great possibility.

Politics and diplomacy are now used for gain. America and Europe are coming together with some Asian countries to punish Russia. Humanity is not ready for political union to create benevolence. Politics and diplomacy are about mischief. Humans are not ready. Businesses share the common goal of making money. Uniting all countries is to their advantage.

I have heard that there are American colonies on Mars and that humans are getting thrown off the Moon. Is this true?

I will say only one thing: There is a civilization on Mars that lives underground, and there is also a civilization that lives under the surface of the Moon. Governments will attempt to mine the Moon, colonize it, and claim ownership of it. The winner takes all.

But there are other aliens on the Moon, aren't there?

Yes, definitely. Even on Mars.

Blessings. This is Archangel Michael.

• • •

Anchor Absolute Courage

Hello, my name is Erelim. I am the angel who supports courage, valor, and the strength not to fight but to be courageous in your life situations. It is only when you are courageous that you are able to make changes and take action. All the great inventors and explorers have been supported by my energy. They had fear in their hearts. They were going to unknown places, but they held the conviction that going there could make a difference.

When you are courageous, you can dare to do new things. Even when life is difficult, you can stand up, and say, "Yes it is tough. I might even lose my home, but I can get another." Courage can enhance all aspects of your life immensely, not only your spiritual practice.

Most people are not courageous at all. They may pretend to be. But deep down, they are not courageous. They are afraid of change. I work with people to have courage in the unknown. It is courage in the unknown that will propel you to take the next step and to have faith.

All great masters walked alone. They had their convictions, and they were courageous. They knew their paths came from their souls with the support of their guides and the Creator. They followed their paths. They had the courage to stand in the truth of their souls. Even if they lost their lives, they lived their truth. Jesus had this courage. When he was persecuted, he never wavered.

We ask you to come to this place. You can call on me to anchor the energy of absolute courage into you — the courage to know your truth and to live your truth. Courage also means you can change your truth because it is your creation. You believe in yourself and your inner power to create the life you want. The world may not understand you. You will go forth and not rest until you find yourself fully. Brother Robert, do you have this courage within you?

Speaker 2: Probably not.

Speaker 3: I think I do now.

Speaker 4: I think this was a very important message for me. My courage has been waning, but I feel supported now.

Speaker 5: I feel the same way. It gives me courage to have courage.

Speaker 6: I agree with having the courage to have courage. It is something we want; we just need to remind ourselves that we have this, and I am there.

Everyone is born with immense courage. But through life experiences and how you are raised, you forget this quality.

You will see more and more people awakening, and there will be a need for many more masters to guide them. When this awakening happens, the exact opposite will also happen because we live in a dualistic world. You are here to master both aspects, the light and the dark. You cannot put on rose-colored glasses and say that the world is full of light. There is evil; there is darkness. You are here to master both aspects. When there is awakening, the other side will open up more.

There will be more messages of fear. More darkness will come. Because you worked through the darkness within yourself, when you can stand in your truth, you will be able to help others do the same so that they will be courageous enough to seek their truth, find their truth, live their truth, and experience their truth. In this, you will raise the vibration immensely, for it is said that courage and truth are next to God.

We ask you to activate this energy within you. We can support you with this. This energy is located in your sexual organs, both female and male. This energy is called tabolic energy, and it is orange in color.

Close your eyes, bring your attention to your sexual organs, and see this space being filled with beautiful orange light. You do not have to do anything. Just give attention to this orange light. This orange light will start moving. It might fill that part of your body with orange light. It might contract. It might change. It will have some sacred geometric patterns. Just be with this orange light.

The light might suddenly shoot up through you and into your arms, or it might go back down. Maybe it will go into your toes, or maybe it will go into your eyes. Just be with this orange light. Allow it to move in any way.

The orange light might move into the back of your shoulders, for this is the place of the energy of fear, right underneath your shoulder blades. The color is soft gray. This is the energy of fear in the human body because your karmic chakras are in the shoulders. Sometimes the orange light will shoot to this place, and the gray will disappear in a small ball of orange light. This ball will not stay. It will go back to the place where it began [the sexual organs]. This is the place where it is located all the time. Let it move anywhere it wants to move.

Once you become familiar with this energy, you will be able to move it anywhere you want, especially to the back of your shoulders where it can disperse a lot of fear. Now see the energy going back where it started, like a small orange dot in your sexual organs. Breathe it, and then just be there. You may open your eyes at this time and share what you feel.

I was surprised that the energy was located in the second chakra. I was expecting it to be somewhere else. And the idea that the color of fear is gray resonated very deeply. I think I'm going to be able to use that again. I feel that very powerfully.

It can make a difference, especially when you have courage. This is an entirely new way of thinking. You are no longer in survival mode. You are self-reliant. Your consciousness is self-sufficient, and you can create again. You do not automatically operate from survival consciousness. When that happens, there is a huge shift. Would anybody else like to share?

With the energy of fear stored between the shoulders, is that why so many people have stiff shoulders?

Yes, combined with their karmic energy. You store your karmic energy in your back.

I could feel the orange energy moving around, and I also can say that so many of my clients have stiff, burdened shoulders. It makes a lot of sense to me to hear that this is fear based.

How does a confident person walk?

Erect.

A confident person will always walk erect, and you can see a confident human being.

I found that as we did the meditation, it went to different areas of my body where I hold fear. I thought about my clients who have great pain underneath their scapulas, which is very difficult to address. I am thinking about bringing the orange light when I put my hands on them.

Yes. Here is another thing for people who are in healing professions: Once you activate this energy within you, program the intention of this energy into your crystal. Then you can touch the back of your clients with the crystal and transmit this energy into their backs.

Christine and I both use tuning forks, and we could program the crystals with the turning forks.

Of course. Thank you, family.

This is Angel Erelim.

• • •

Divine Your Future

Hello, dear ones. This is Archangel Michael. Most of you are interested in knowing about the potentials for your life. People in all cultures have been going to others to know about the future from time immemorial. Kings employed them throughout history. Now channels have been able to tap into a different reality.

There is an angel who can support you, an angel of divination, to help you with the ability to see far into the future and make changes. We are honored this angel is speaking with us.

• • •

Hello, my name is Eisiti [pronounced Ee-See-Tee]. I am the principal carrier of the energy called divination. I worked with the oracles of Delphi, and I influenced the first oracles who lived there in a cave [the cave of Parnassus, near Delphi, Greece]. Brother Rae and Brother Robert had an opportunity to visit this cave during their travels [May 2014].

I ask you to connect with my energy, and you will become your own master. You will be able to see your future clearly and accurately. Combine the colors metallic green and metallic lavender into your auric field and into the soles of your feet and your fingers. There are many energies there to support you in everyday life. People rarely see these parts of their bodies as having consciousness. The energetic points in your fingers and toes (and throughout your feet) have the potential to open your understanding of the future.

How does this work? Your feet are on the ground. You walk on the ground every day. Your future is directly encoded with Gaia's energy. You plant the future into the ground through your feet so that it is manifested as a reality on her body and comes back into your life.

To know your future, focus on your feet, for you draw your future through your feet from the ground. You manifest that reality. In this way, the players in your life manifest to create situations that bring you awareness, lessons, karmic closure, and healing. A similar thing happens with your hands, for they are the means by which you take action. Through action, you are creating a reality. Your hands and feet play a very big role in knowing about your future.

Call on me to ask for my energy to be anchored into these parts of your body using beautiful metallic green and metallic purple colors. You will feel an energy imprinted into your hands, legs, and soles. These energetic imprints will create sacred geometric patterns, especially in your feet. These patterns will be imbedded in the ground when you walk. You will know exactly what is happening or what kinds of seeds you are putting down to create your own future reality.

It is a beautifully designed system. Are you ready to know your future? Call on me, Eisiti. I am the angel of divination.

Does it matter whether we are wearing shoes or walking barefoot?

Barefoot is best, and leather shoes are second best. If this is not possible, rubber shoes are okay. If you walk with bare feet, you will feel more clearly the energy and the patterns of the sacred geometry being formed in the ground.

We understand that if you are living in a cold place, you cannot put your feet on the ground. Just give the intention that the energy you are anchoring from your hands and feet goes through the soles of your feet into the ground.

How do you feel about divining rods? I use them sometimes.

All divination tools came from me. You can ask that the future you are creating be revealed to you through your feet. You will see that you will become your own master of divination.

We will feel the future through our impressions?

Exactly. When you start anchoring energy into your hands and feet, we work with your soul and your I Am presence. The new energy that we anchor into the ground creates a new sacred geometrical pattern. This will be in resonance with your soul. What you create will often not only be from your mind but also from a higher perspective. This will help you to move onto the path of your soul.

It is now clear to me what our intention should be with our feet, but do you have any advice about what we should do with our hands, like mudras?

Hold your thumb, index, and middle fingers together for both hands. Bring them in front of your solar plexus. When we channel the energy, you work with your chakras too.

This is Angel Eisiti. Good day, and blessings to you. I will be waiting for all of you.

• • •

Would the energy moving up from the ground into our feet be more accelerated in Jerusalem because of the energy in the ground there?

This is Archangel Michael. When you are in a powerful spot on Mother Earth's body that has power nodes or power vortexes, the energy is amplified, and you are able to feel it more — if you are in a state of readiness to feel the energy. The same is true at Mount Shasta. If you are in a state of readiness, then you will feel it more, for the energy will be amplified.

CHAPTER FOUR

Access Support from Celestial Bodies

Angel Noguel, Angel Nakhiel, Angel Guth, Angel Chismael, Archangel Metatron, Angel of Spinal Column Fluid, Archangel Michael, La Banaha, Master Jesus, and Lord Shiva

Hello. My name is Noguel. I am the head angel who supports the planet Venus. Venus is a very important planet in how it supports humanity. Venus is a jumping place before you come into the Earth plane. It is the place where many of you said goodbye to your loved ones, guides, and others.

There is alignment of stars and planets for each person. We are not talking about astrological alignments. Different star systems and planets align with each other to support everyone on the Earth plane. Venus is one of these planets. The master of Venus is Master Sanat Kumara.

Love and Support from Home

There are planetary lines going around your physical body. From your foot to your head, you have twelve circles around you, each representing a different color, vibration, and planetary energies. In the middle of your body, just above your navel, see a soft-purple circle of light about two inches wide. It is like a tube around your body, and it has many holes from which are pouring beautiful soft-purple colors. Breathe in these colors, and in your mind's eye, see yourself filled with them. You have become a beautiful soft-purple-colored being.

If you do this daily, your connection with the planet Venus will become much stronger. Venus is the place where you feel most comfortable, where you are with your loved ones, higher self, council of creators who support your present creation, guides, teachers, and everyone else. It is truly a place of home for you.

When you start connecting with Venus's energy, you will be able to feel at home more than you are feeling now, and you will have a sense of great love and support. This is your true family. Slowly, you will start to awaken to the memory of your prebirth contracts, classes, counseling, and guidance from your guides and teachers. I can support you in this. Humanity will awaken to this truth, and they will feel the love of their councils, their supporting energies, that they felt before they were born. This is the unconditional love you all seek.

Thank you. Is it possible to give us information about a few of the other major planets, such as Sirius or Orion? I understand I'm mainly from Sirius, so that interests me.

We will see whether the beings who support these energetic imprints can speak with you in the future. They have their own angelic presence and support teams for each planet.

You are for Venus only?

Yes, for Venus. We mentioned Venus first because Venus is your true home. You have other planets, but Venus is a place where you gather with all your loved ones, guides, and your support teams. It is a gathering place of love, friendship, laughter, and fun before you are brought here.

Earth is the sister planet of Venus?

Yes, Earth is a planetary testing ground. Before you go on an expedition, you have a big celebration with all your loved ones to honor you. We ask you to be aware of these energies and connect with them. Blessings. I must say, this has been very short.

• • •

Hello, my name is Nakhiel. I am connected to the Central Sun and directly connected to your Sun. There has been much channeling and understanding brought forth about using the Sun's rays and about the individual rays of the Sun for each human being. As you know, the Sun is very important. Without the Sun, there is no life at all.

Some scriptures say the sun chakra is in the solar plexus, which is true. Can you say that it is only the solar plexus that holds the Sun's energy? I am sure you know it is not. The Sun shines in every part of the body.

There are many miniature suns around your own Sun, but because of the brilliance of the Sun's light, they cannot be seen. This is understood by just a handful of people on the planet.

Connect with the Sun to Become One with Everything

Many planets and many masters have twelve beings supporting them — the power of twelve. Master Buddha had twelve disciples called Little Buddhas. Melchizedek had twelve disciples called Melchizedek Disciples. In the same way, there are twelve miniature suns supporting the Sun. These twelve beings are part of your energetic field, and you can connect with them and through them to the energy of the Sun.

Now close your eyes, dear family. Imagine that you are wearing a beautiful, white, one-inch belt around your stomach. There are twelve suns attached to this white belt going around your waist. Just breathe this in, and see the energy from the belt going into your stomach. The energy of six of these suns goes upward and the energy of six goes downward. Six go into your left hand, and six go into your right hand. Visualize this as best as you can. Just breathe it in one more time. Breathe it in. Breathe it in.

When you start doing this on a regular basis, you will see the twelve planets that are around us. You will feel the energy of these planets within your being.

You have heard many times that the universe lives within you, but why are you not able to feel it? If the planets are part of you, why do you not feel them? Incorporate these twelve miniature suns within you. They will increase your vibration. You will become a being who holds all twelve planets within you. You will become the Milky Way.

Breathe again. [Pause.] One more time [pause], and one more time. Now open your eyes.

How do you feel?

Speaker 1: I feel quite expanded.

Speaker 2: Lifted.

Speaker 3: Expanded.

After practicing this for a few weeks, you will start feeling the movement of the planets within your physical body. Your body holds the vibration of the twelve planets. Not only will you expand your consciousness, but you will also bring a large part of the universe into yourself. Once you start connecting with these planets moving harmoniously inside you, all the other things supported by these planetary movements will slowly come into your being — such as the elements and energetic life forms. You will slowly start to feel that the universe exists within you and that you are part of it: "I am one with the universe. I am the universe." The key to this is the twelve miniature suns that support you.

When you start sending the energy of six suns above your navel and six below as well as six in your left hand and six in your right hand, you will also activate many other chakras in those parts of your body. Your hands hold two different vibrational energies. One hand holds the energy for all animal species. The other hand holds the template and vibrational patterns of energy for all kinds of plants.

We ask you to close your eyes again, and focus on the belt around your body with the twelve miniature suns full of bright light. This is like twelve rivets of sun on your belt. See this belt rotating in your mind's eye. It is not static. It is going around your body.

Beams of light from the twelve suns are beamed into your body, going up and down, six above and six below, like streams of light. Direct six lights into your left hand and six into your right hand. Ask that all your connections with the plants and trees be fully activated in your left hand. Ask that all your connections with the animal beings (including animals living in the water) be activated in your right hand. Bring your attention to the palms of your hands and the tips of your fingers. Breathe three times.

What this does is begin the experience of feeling the planets inside you. Then you will start feeling the life forms that exist on the Earth plane within your being. You will begin to truly experience the oneness with all creation within your physical body — first the planets, then the life force energy that already exists on the planet, like plants, animals, and all other forms of creation.

Breathe again [pause] and again [pause] and one more time. Gently open your eyes.

We are bringing all of you to the level of experiencing creation fully within your physical body. This has been a challenge for people: "If we are part of the whole, why are we not able to feel the whole within us, including the planets and every life form?" How do you feel?

Speaker 2: I feel something along the line of what you just said, about participating in the creation, with little pinpricks of light in my hands, and how this integrates us into the whole universe. It's quite marvelous. "Marvelous" is a poor word, but it is how I feel.

Speaker 1: I feel like I'm bursting with this incredible activity and the joyfulness of creation. I feel as if I am participating in the creation of life.

This is called I Am That I Am: "I am the planets. I am the spirit of all living beings, the animals and plants, and I can experience this in my physical body, just from the miniature suns." Work with these twelve miniature suns, and you will see marvel after marvel appearing in your life. Sometimes you will be floating, and you will say, "My God, this is magic." Yes, it is magic, and you are a magician.

I'm really intrigued by the twelve miniature suns.

If you study your Torah really deeply, you will see them referred to. Why do we have twelve spheres? Why do we have the power of twelve? Why do we have so many twelves?

Why do we have twelve tribes? Understood. Are these miniature suns ethereal, or can they actually be seen?

They can actually be seen; however, only through the spiritual eye.

Most astronomers would not be able to see them.

It is not in their perception of reality to even think that such things exist. Believing is seeing. The more you believe, the more is revealed to you.

They are not in this dimension. Is that a correct statement?

They are in this dimension.

But people who activate their spiritual sight would be able to see them?

Yes, only then. Otherwise, they would say you need to go to a shrink to get your head checked.

You mentioned Melchizedek with his twelve disciples. Do all sages, teachers, and ascended masters have twelve disciples under them?

Not everyone, but some do who are teachers. They have twelve because the twelve carry out the work of the great master. For the Sun, there are miniature suns; for the masters, there are miniature masters.

Initiation with the Earth and the Sky

There are certain exercises you can do to connect with the twelve miniature suns. This is best done on a warm, sunny day. This may not be possible in the United States at this time because of the weather, but for brother Mordechai, it is always possible to do this.

You will want to do this outside on the ground if possible. Draw a circle. It could be a small circle on the ground, maybe half a meter in diameter. Put twelve earthen pots around the circle, and fill them with twelve elements from the earth. What is of the earth is grown underground. You could use a piece of a potato or carrot plant, for instance. Next, add twelve elements of the sky. By "sky," I mean a flower that grows in the ground, but once it opens and blooms, it is blooming and showing itself to the sky. You can call ripe cotton an element from the sky. Fill the pots up with twelve elements from the sky and twelve from the earth. Natural things from the earth are grown in the earth and remain in the ground completely. Some show their tops to the light, and some do not. This is the main difference.

You have twelve elements of the earth and twelve elements of sky. Mix them and burn them very lightly. They may not fully burn, but they will smoke. Draw a triangle in the center of the circle and make a Star of David in this triangle. Dig a very small hole in the ground and symbolically pass your hands over the pots. You symbolically collect the energy from the twelve pots and deposit it into the ground, into the hole you have made. Just be there and breathe it into you.

This symbolizes your initiation with the earth and sky. Your body is of Mother Earth. This will balance the energy within you, and you will be able to feel warmth or heat from these twelve earthen pots. They represent the twelve miniature suns. This is best done in an open, outside place.

Blessings. This is Angel Nakhiel. Call on me to support you, for I am the spiritual angel supporting the Sun.

• • •

Hello, my friends. I am Guth. I am an angel supporting the great benevolent planet you call Jupiter. All of you know me as a Santa Claus who brings presents for people. But why wait for Santa Claus on your Christmas Eve? Why not make it every day? Are you not worthy of my gifts? Many people believe they are worthy, but when their gifts come, they think something is wrong. We are here to assist humanity, and if called forth, we will be there.

Human beings carry the energetic vibrations of all twelve planets[1] with them. You can consciously access these vibrations by calling them forth and requesting their energy to be enhanced. Consider the twelve planets and their functions: They are fully conscious beings, and they respond to your communication, especially if it comes from your heart. Ask that their energy be enhanced. For example, Saturn is a taskmaster. We want to bring the lessons to you, but you can ask the essence of Saturn to reduce the intensity. You can ask me, an angel for Jupiter, to enhance the energy of Jupiter within you so that more gifts come into your life.

What I am here to say is not about me. It is time for you to start looking at how to work with the planets by communicating and requesting. For example,

1. A Google search results in different versions of the twelve planets, for example, Mercury, Venus, Earth, Mars, Ceres, Jupiter, Saturn, Uranus, Neptune, Pluto, Charon, and 2003 UB 313. Astro.com lists the twelve planets as Mercury, Venus, Earth, Mars, Ceres, Jupiter, Saturn, Uranus, Neptune, Pluto, Charon, and 2003 UP 313 (provisional name).

there are twelve scales in music, but you do not play all the scales at once. Sometimes you play one scale to enhance a vibration or sound that you want to bring forth. In the same way, you can ask and make a direct connection with a planet, and your life will become much easier.

My message is very simple and short, but I think you get the point. Has it not been told to you again and again? All energies exist within you, and when you give intention to experience the energy that already exists within you, you are in a very powerful place.

I have a verification question. I know that the editor at the publisher is going to ask me this. You mentioned twelve planets. Could you say what those are, because I'm only familiar with nine.

It's very easy. Look into that. Do you know the meaning of "Google," brother? You will find it. One day, there will be an opportunity for all the twelve planets to speak. When a human being comes to understand the twelve planets fully, along with their functions in the human body, the thirteenth planet will appear. Blessings, brother. We are joking with you; you know that.

I know. I've been roundly chastised!

Now you know that you can strengthen what you want strengthened and reduce the intensity of what you do not want to experience. That is a basic one-line message from me.

This is Guth, beloved uncle for people of Earth, friend of Santa and all good things in life.

• • •

Call Forth the Seeds You've Planted in Other Lifetimes

Hello, family, what a beautiful time to be interacting with you. My name is Angel Chismael. I am an angel supporting the planet you know as Jupiter. Everyone wants to be friends with Jupiter, for Jupiter is like Santa Claus bringing forth gifts, if you are ready. Every planet has its own support system of angels (and others).

Jupiter plays a very big role in your life. Every planet has a certain influence and function in your life, but how would you like to have Jupiter in your life on a more constant basis? Jupiter is the bringer of the fruits of your work. That means that if you have put in the effort with proper intentions, then the benefits are there for you. In simple words, if you have sown the proper seeds and taken care of the land, you will have a good harvest.

People do not understand that Jupiter has the capacity to bring forth gifts not only from what you have sown in this lifetime but from other lifetimes as well. Jupiter does not have a timeframe like you do. But because of the limitations you have brought when coming to this planet, Jupiter is not able to bring forth gifts from past lives. You often receive the benefit and gifts from Jupiter from your efforts in this lifetime. Now you can ask to be open and ready to receive gifts from other lifetimes. Can you imagine the seeds you have planted in other lifetimes? Most people do not even think of such things. This can change your life immediately and immensely.

You have worked hard in this lifetime to find solace and peace in your hearts with whatever you have created for yourself. You have planted many seeds. Some have germinated; some have not. After a certain time, you pass away. In your next lifetime, you will start again from the bottom and struggle. How would you like to have the seeds that you planted in this lifetime bloom in your next lifetime? You may not know what seeds you have planted, but your soul knows. You can simply ask that all the seeds you planted in other lifetimes (especially in the past three lifetimes on the Earth plane) be brought forth.

Chismael, I love your perspective as being the galactic Santa Claus. You fill the bags. Can you tell me who delivers them? Do you wear another hat as the deliverer of the gifts?

I am in partnership with the spirit of Jupiter. I would say we are one. The gifts are delivered through strong intuitive feelings and inspiration that you cannot deny.

How do you choose which gifts to give us?

We do not choose. We look at what you have done in other lifetimes, what seeds you have planted, and your intention behind planting the seeds. Then we bring that forth, especially if it is for the highest good and is a part of your soul. Almost all the time, we bring forth gifts that have been asked for.

When you say "inspiration and feeling," would enthusiasm be the key?

Receiving is the key, the ability to receive and take inspired actions. When strong feelings come, you must act on them. Although you may say, "I never attempted to do that in this lifetime," the gifts are coming from other lifetimes when you planted the seeds. Even when you die, the energy of what you planted can still be manifested in the future.

Are you saying that the seed is planted in a program of incarnations and that it will blossom when it is needed?

It will blossom when it is nurtured properly. Let us say that you are working hard, and you have planted many seeds. Then you die in a few years. Do you think what you planted has gone to waste? Of course not. If you become aware and open in your next incarnation, you will be able to reap the benefit of what you have sown. It need not be only a linear progression from one lifetime to the next. It could be a continuous life stream of gifts coming from many lifetimes.

How do some people write books or create music? Do you think it is only because of what happened in one lifetime? Of course not. It comes from many lifetimes. They have planted seeds. This is especially relevant for a scientist. When scientists make breakthroughs, do you think it is because of the hard work of one lifetime alone? No, they have been working on the problems in other lifetimes. Now they bloom, and they are ready for their gifts.

During your meditation time, call forth the seeds you have planted in other lifetimes that can support you in your present lifetime. Bring those fruits into your present reality.

• • •

This is Archangel Metatron. Precious family, we are bringing you practical applications and practical tools. Work with them, and we guarantee your life will never be the same. How can you teach others unless first you have practiced yourself? See whether using these tools supports you in your life. Then you will be authentic when you say, "I used this, and I worked with it. It changed my life. I am a new being now."

Look at all the past lives you have had, all that you have achieved, and all the efforts you have made. It is time to reap what you have sown. Look at this lifetime. You attended to so many things with blood, sweat, and tears. Some did not materialize. But they may materialize in another lifetime, for the seed is planted deep. You can go back and ask that all the seeds you planted in all the areas of your life you wanted to improve, change, or create be brought forth in your present lifetime. You will see dramatic changes in your life, and enhanced abilities will come to you. You will have a sense of, "Hmm, I got it. I can feel it."

Make Jupiter your best friend, for he is ready to open and share new gifts.

Work with Planets and the Karmic Board

There are many planets in service to you, supporting you. Some planets bring benevolent support, and some planets bring a lesson forth to be completed. Some planets are balanced in both. If you are going through a challenging time, you can say, "I give intent to enter the energy of the planet Venus, for Venus is a place that is very familiar to you. It is from Venus that you came to the Earth plane, and from Venus, you bid farewell to your guides and friends. It was a place of comfort before you took the big journey.

Venus is a place of celebration, great peace, and great beauty. You can ask to be taken there whenever you need a boost of energy. It is also a place of many masters. There is only absolute love there. Make it a habit of going there every two or three days. You will feel nurtured and uplifted, and perhaps you will start remembering more of your life path and why you came to Earth.

There are interdimensional temples on Venus and elsewhere where you can ask for liquid love. Love can be liquefied in other dimensions. Many people on Earth are given this potion by their guides. You may wonder how people can survive harsh conditions such as prison. During their deep sleep, they are given liquid love so that they can complete what they have come here to do. You can consciously ask for this to be given to you. Since it contains such a high vibration of pure love, it will expand inside of you. You will feel more loving. When you start doing this, it will start triggering many things inside of you because it is coming from the place of pure love itself.

This high love energy activates pure love inside of you. That opens many portals, and great healing can take place. Higher energies can come through these portals to support you. You will feel good about yourself. Ask for this consciously. Create an intention notebook and write in it, "I visited the temple of love, and I requested that liquid love be given to me." This is especially good for people who are having difficult times, who live alone, or who feel lonely and that no one loves them. The greatest force is love — to be loved and to love in return.

Schedule Meetings with the Karmic Board

Every week or every month, write in your intention book that you will meet with the Karmic Board. When you meet regularly with the Karmic Board, a bond is created. Your remaining karmic energy can be dispersed or transmuted with their help.

So much energy from the ancient past is coming forward now. There is so much ugliness at this time. When you go to the Karmic Board, many deep-seated, deeply buried karmic energies can be shifted, healed, or changed. This is similar to criminals who go before a parole board. A parole board evaluates the criminals' situations, whether they are working on themselves, how much they have changed, and whether they have taken courses to improve their lives. The Karmic Board does not look at the scenarios of your life. You bring these lessons forward yourself.

The Karmic Board looks at how you are handling your life. Are you working to heal yourself? The Karmic Board most often looks at your work and your energy. Ask that the karmic energies still existing within you be moved forward, shifted, or reduced in intensity. Do this regularly. Make them your friends, and they will respond to you. They are very much in touch with you, and they want you to communicate and begin a dialogue. They will give you some practical tools to work with.

When coming before the Karmic Board, will they present situations to us to be healed? Or do we go to them and ask about specific situations in our lives?

Ask them specifically. They will project thoughts and images into your mind about the situation you are going through — what you can do about it, what your real intention is, and what the real issue is. They look at the results. Are you working on it? That is the key question for them. They want you to do work on this issue. The Karmic Board members are very loving, kind beings. Expect gentleness from them. They just want to balance the energy, and that is all. They will guide you to where you need to balance the energy, where you need to put your energy, where you need to push your energy, where you need to give energy, and where you need to pull back energy.

Saturn Can Help You Through Hard Times

If you are having a hard time in your life, you can call on the great master Saturn. Ask how you can learn and gain wisdom from the difficult experiences you are going through with less intensity. This planet will respond to you. Some planets are not tough taskmasters. They are looking at how much wisdom you have gained. Ask Saturn to show you wisdom about your health or financial issues. Ask about the wisdom you can gain from these experiences.

All the planets will communicate now. They have been communicating, but now they are much more active because the Creator is much more active in this present reality. Every being and every essence in support of humanity is also fully active and offers immediate cooperation to help you.

The people of Earth need our support. The world is becoming more polarized. How can you live in a polarized world? Only by being nonpolarized yourselves. That is all. You cannot change the world, but you can stay nonpolarized and send love to those who need it desperately — the poor, suffering masses. Everything is coming to a head because Earth is purging and cleansing herself. You will see more ugliness. It is not over, and it will not be over for some time. It is going to get more and more intense. Any questions from anybody?

The Karmic Board teaches you how to balance energy; that is all. They do not judge you. Religion has taught you that you are bad. This is wrong. They are basically administrators balancing energy to save humanity; that is all. Are they strict? This depends on your point of view on what is strict. You cannot escape your karma. You need to work on it. They just need to see you working on it. Are there any other questions?

I believe that people in North America are being poisoned by absolute falsehoods through the media. Will that ever change, or are Americans just going to be told more falsehoods through the media?

Right now, things are pointing toward more media falsehoods. This will take some time to shift. Things are going to get uglier before they get better, by 2019 or 2020. You will see more ugliness and more secrets revealed as well as more manipulation by the media. There will be more polarization, so you must remain nonjudgmental and nonpolarized. If you fear the polarization, then you are energizing the polarization.

Last summer [2014], an incident happened near Saint Louis in which a black young man was killed [Ferguson, Missouri].[2] People carried signs and expressed their opinions and outrage. But does any of this resolve the issue? Of course not. It is very easy to get carried away. It is better to stay nonpolarized in your heart, and from that space, your light can engulf everyone.

It is important to remember that you cannot resolve a problem with the same energy with which it was created. It must be resolved in a different way. The test of mastery comes from these situations. Remember, on some level, you are all children of God acting out your karmic energies. It is not for us to judge. You can support others and heal them by holding the light for them.

• • •

Create a Bridge to Other Realities

I am the Angel of Spinal Column Fluid. Humans carry this precious essence in their spinal columns. Your spinal column is truly your bridge to other realities. Create this bridge. You will use it in this lifetime and in other lifetimes. How is

2. For details about the Michael Brown shooting, see http://en.wikipedia.org/wiki/Shooting_of_Michael_Brown.

this your bridge? Is it strong enough? Has it ever been used? Does it need any repairs?

Ask the essence of you spinal column fluid to be pushed upward, through intention and visualization, and see it going through the back of your body, activating the Flower of Life in the back and the torus energy, going all the way back to the ascension chakra and all the way to the crown chakra.

This fluid has many properties. It contains the past, the present, and the future. When you work with this fluid daily and direct it as you want, you will be able to manipulate the flow of this fluid and even change its contents. You will shift your reality.

Many of you have said that you have been working on your spiritual journey for the past forty years: "I did 'this,' and I did 'that,' but I am truly not able to stay in another reality more than momentarily. Rarely can I stay there for more than five minutes."

The key is in the fluid of your spinal column. See it like a fountain shooting up every day. When you wake up in the morning, make the intention that this fountain is shooting upward. You might feel a little spaced-out initially, like you are falling down, because it will crisscross and move in different ways. You will connect with other realities much more quickly. When you start moving this fluid, you are also strengthening your spinal column. Many ancient energies are dormant there. There are many Earths, many dimensions, and many realities you have experienced. All are stored there.

When you start moving your spinal fluid upward, you will condense these energies, bringing all the different realities of Earth into one unified force field. This is why spinal column fluid is such an important part of your life.

There are also energies you call devas living inside your spinal column. You have devas, or energies (sometimes called mini gods), in your chakras. You also have devas inside your spinal column. Call these devas forth. Ask for this activation, pull up this energy, for these devas will support you in pulling this energy upward.

First, we will give you the name of someone to help you with this. We ask you to meditate on this name to see whether you feel good doing so, for this deva (or goddess) is very powerful. Her name is Kamoshi. In your meditation, ask whether you are ready to work with this deva.

When you start pushing the fluid in your spinal column, all your past karmic energy will burn as if it were in an incinerator. This could be painful to your body. It could also be very smooth. Before you do this, ask whether it is good for you to connect with this great goddess and whether you are courageous enough to take this journey.

I would be grateful for you to review the path that we are to take when we push the spinal column fluid upward. You mentioned several chakras, and I was unable to write them all down.

Of course, it affects the chakras in the back of the body, the Flower of Life in the back of the body, the energy of the torus, the back of the neck, and the ascension chakra. Then go into the middle of the head.

You must ask one important question: "Am I ready to work with this goddess?" for this goddess is powerful. She is the power.

Is this practice related to raising the kundalini?

No, it is quite different.

• • •

Kundalini

This is Archangel Michael. We said before we started this book that we would be bringing forth new understandings and new angels, not the ones people already knew, but completely new angelic beings who support humanity.

It is difficult to raise the kundalini because it is combined with many forces. The energies of the chakras determine how the kundalini is moved. It takes people many, many lifetimes to come to a place of being able to move this energy. Now we are bringing forth understanding that can move it much faster and without the hardships.

For example, let us say that you are constructing a house one hundred years ago. How were homes constructed then? Brick by brick. How was cement mixed? By hand. You used a trowel to spread the cement, and then you placed a brick. Again, you used a trowel to spread the cement, and then you placed a brick. How do you do this today? A big machine comes, and it lays out tons of bricks continuously.

We are saying yes, you can raise the kundalini, but if it were easy, why have many more people not raised it? Because it is not easy. Now, there is a new consciousness. Things can be done differently. Now you have new tools and new technology to make life much easier. Does that mean the old system is obsolete? I would say no. Depending on their belief systems, some people say, "I need to go through this process." So we honor that.

Okay. That helps me understand it. The new process is like a laptop computer. It's just a lot faster and works better.

It is a choice. People can choose between a laptop or a 1950s room-sized mainframe.

This is like steppingstones. You have to step on the basic level first before going higher.

• • •

Rejuvenate Your Body with the Moon's Energy

Hello, my friends. I am La Banaha. I am the essence of the great one you call the Moon. I am the mother. I am the essence that runs through you. I am the one who relates directly to your emotional bodies, mental bodies, feeling bodies, and spiritual bodies, as well as your light. I am with you from the time of your conception until the end of your life. But very little is understood about me. I have come here not to tell my story but to tell you how to utilize me and work with me so that you can once again be an empowered human being.

This is the age of empowerment. In this age of empowerment, you must consciously ask, "What are the things I can work with to be in a state of empowerment?" The tools I give you today will help. But you must also be aware that your mental and emotional bodies have a grip on you that is strong and difficult to break.

We ask all of you to place your dominant hand (right or left) on your solar plexus, for this is where I reside inside you. This is a place of immense power. This is a midway point between heaven and Earth within you. Feel me like a coiled snake awakening (a circle within a circle) and spinning, sometimes clockwise and sometimes counterclockwise. [Singing slowly, about five seconds per syllable:] *La Ba Na Ha.*

You will feel me fully in your solar plexus, for I am the force of creation that emanates power. The feminine is stronger, for the feminine creates, and I am the feminine within you. [Singing:] *La Ba Na Ha.* Once you are in this space of incredible power in your solar plexus, you can direct this light to places of healing in your own body, your country, or to Earth. Ask that all the parts of your body be rejuvenated and filled with my incredible power.

Where does your creativity come from? You might think it comes from your mind. Yes, a small portion of it does. It comes from your organs. If your organs are weak, no amount of power will come to your mind. You see this in sick people. If their organs are weak, they are generally weak. If you have a simple cold, you feel miserable. You do not feel your power. Your organs support your mind.

Let all the organs of your body be rejuvenated by my power. This will not just work at the highest level. The organs carry many other properties — healing, creativity — and qualities that can come through you. Many people believe peace can be achieved through their minds. This is a good concept, but why is there no peace in the world? Everything originates in your organs.

Make a list of all the major organs in your body. During your meditation, run my energy into each organ. Say, "My liver. I ask La Banaha to infuse my liver with the La Banaha energy." Be in this space for two to three minutes, and then go to another organ. Do this for a few days. You will be energized.

What happens to people as they grow old? Their bodies lose vitality, and their organs often lose vitality; some organs fail. But if you work with me on a daily basis, you will continuously overhaul and rejuvenate your organs and keep them in pristine condition. This is my invitation to you.

You said that you had different origins. Can you speak a little bit about who you are?

I am La Banaha, the Moon. The Moon was created for a very specific purpose. When the Creator wanted to have a planet as an experiment, many ingredients needed to go into making a planet for humanity. The dragons came first. After that, many other beings, including animals, plants, mammals, and fish, were brought here. If you look at beings who live on this planet now, almost everything is water based. I am the element who regulates the water in everything. I regulate the water in human beings, plants, and animals. Remember, most of your body is water.

Each of your organs has specific vibrational codes that must be activated in order to live in higher-dimensional realities. When a master ascends, what happens? The first shift is in the organs of the body. The organs are able to hold more of the vibration of the master. You often see a master's energy radiating through their eyes because the eyes have shifted to hold the higher vibration. Your organs are the key, for they rule your bodies, your emotional, mental, spiritual, feeling, and light bodies.

Work with this. Work with the creative force from the center of your stomach, and you will truly be tapping into an incredible power source that you cannot even conceive of at this time. That is heaven and Earth. It is like a dam with water behind it. If you lift the gates of a dam, the water flows with incredible force. This is the same thing. I am behind the dam but not acknowledged. When you release the gates of the dam, I am ready to flood you.

How do we work with the solar plexus to support our organs? Do we concentrate and focus our consciousness?

Focus your attention on your solar plexus, and start breathing from there. Ask for La Banaha energy to come through you. You will feel energy coming in; then call my name, La Banaha.

Activate the Moon Chakra to Support the Emotional Body

I am supported by helpers of angelic light. You can also call on them, for they are powerful. They help me to protect my energy fields. You can call on these beings to support you, to protect your own energy field. But like everything else, you must ask.

The energy of the Moon is in your physical body, as well as the energy of the Sun. People have heard about the sun chakra, but who has heard about the moon chakra? The moon chakra is very important because it supports your emotional body.

Where is the moon chakra?

Right in the middle of the forehead.

In the same place as the sixth chakra?

No, above that, further toward the top of the head.

You also have a chakra at the base of your spinal column. The Moon directly affects this chakra too. You have heard about the cerebral fluid in the spinal column? This fluid can be pushed upward. Why is it not easy to push this fluid up? You can work with my angels and my energy because I am (in conventional terms) the master for activating this chakra and the fluids inside the spine.

Every fluid in your body, including saliva, is ready to meet every fluid. You are a fluid being. How can it not be this way? Call on me, and I, with my angels, will help you move this fluid through your spinal column. Utilize me. Let us become friends.

When we move the fluid through our spinal columns, what can we expect?

Many things. You are moving your chi energy, your spiritual body. You are moving it upward. What happens? You activate your torus energy in your back. You activate the blue lotus in your back. You activate and affect your heart. When the fluid goes up, you activate the ascension chakra on your neck when this fluid goes into your brain.

Every fluid in the body is related to me. Ask me to support you in pushing and moving this. We will work together. I cannot do this for you, but we will work together. Your intention, combined with my energy, can help you to push this fluid upward through your spinal column.

Any place and any time there is water, know that I am there. Because you are a water being, how can I not be? I have influence over every bit of water in your body. I am the master. Thank you, dear one. I love you very much.

• • •

Hello, dear family. This is Master Jesus. What we are bringing forth are truly ancient mystery school teachings. In ancient times, this material was only taught to initiates who were ready. When you work with this energy, you are commanding your cells to be whole once again. This is the true meaning of, "I am the resurrection. I am the light. I am the resurrection. I am the light." You are truly resurrecting yourselves into the new you, where the I Am force works within you.

This is a force so powerful that you cannot even conceive it. What happens when I join with you? We speak with one voice. You and your guides are speaking with one voice. You and Creator are speaking with one voice without separation: "I am La Banaha."

• • •

Discover the Illusions of Your Soul

This is Lord Shiva. I am delighted that you are so receptive to this high level of mystery teachings. It is a joy to share with you. I will pose some questions to you. I will not give you the answers. This is homework.

Write this on a piece of paper: "Illusions of the mind are rather easy. Illusions of the body are also rather easy. What about illusions of the soul? What are my soul's illusions?" Undertaking this quest sincerely and earnestly can liberate you.

One part of your body is very important. You use it many times every day. This is your urinary tract. You go to the bathroom to pass water. You drink water, and you pass it. Have you ever wondered what you are passing? You might say it is the waste from your body. This is true. But the water inside you contains great truths and great secrets about you. Every time you go to the bathroom, you unconsciously dilute this truth and release it through your body. Does this mean that you should not go to the bathroom? Of course not.

When you were born, there were truths about you in the water of your body that could set you free. But through your elimination system, these qualities have been lost. When you drink a glass of water, it does not contain your original intention for this lifetime.

You can work with La Banaha and go to Venus. Ask that your original intention, the content and the essence of the water inside you when you were born, be restored. Say, "I anchor this intention in my solar plexus, so when I urinate, I will not release it." When you make this request, it is granted. This is a simple but very powerful tool. If you work with this technique, it can dramatically affect your life.

This was created so that you would forget why you were born. Now you can go back and ask for your original intention to be restored, and you will not lose it because you tie it to your solar plexus. Whatever energy you want, tie it to your solar plexus. Enlarge it and work with it every week. Who can do this for you? La Banaha. She is the force. She is the one who nurtures you inside your mother's womb.

You are a water being. When you were born, you became an air being. The connection to water was cut off. Now you can ask that your original intention as a water being be replaced once a day. Spiritually, it is already set; there is nothing to learn, only to remember. You can go back and say, "I lost it, and I am going to replace it."

Is this difficult? I do not think so. Ask, and it shall be given. This is Shiva.

CHAPTER FIVE

Invoke Vibrational Support and Activation

Archangel Michael, Angel Nibra Ha Rishon, Lord Shiva, Angel Tahariel, the Violet Angel, Lily Angel, Archangel Metatron, Archangel Tadzekiel, and Angel Suria

This is Archangel Michael. Following, we have an exceptionally powerful and wise angel. Why do I say "exceptional"? There is no hierarchy among angels. But like everyone else, angels vibrate at different levels, so there is a sort of hierarchy among angels and archangels. The angel who will speak with you next carries one of the highest vibrations, and he can be called to support you to raise your vibration and to expand your capacity to hold more light.

• • •

Blessings and love to my dear family and to the family of Earth, for many in the family of Earth will read my words in the future. This is the present for me. My name is Nibra Ha Rishon. I am an emissary of the Creator. I visit planets, star systems, and galaxies to gauge their evolution and movement. You have school district officers who visit schools to see how they are doing. Sometimes, they step into a class to see how they are being taught and whether the students are responsive. They look at how the tests are administered. You also have tax inspectors visiting companies: Are they complying, are they growing, and are they paying?

In all walks of life, people gauge the evolution of businesses, schools, and other things. There are also angels and other beings who gauge the consciousness of a planet or whether a planet or star system is growing. I head that council.

Miles to Go before You Sleep

As you know, there is much focus on your planet because of what has happened and who you are. I do not want to go into the details because you know who you are and your purpose for being here. I have come to give you some encouragement and to tell you that you are on the right path. You are coming along pretty well, but there is much work yet to be done. This is not new. You are aware of this. Being with the angels can help you increase your vibration at a much faster rate than you have ever experienced up to this time in your reality.

My energy group sends vibrational energy into your planet. We have seen the planet increase its vibration and drop again, going up and down. This time, we do not intend for the vibration to drop again, and the people of Earth will be able to get up and move forward.

We beam a red light into your planet. You can call for this red light to maintain your vibrational energy at a certain frequency. You work to build a certain frequency, but when you go out into the world and are confronted with its problems, your energy level drops. You are not able to maintain it. This is a critical key to moving forward. You must be able to maintain and increase your vibration constantly. This is where we come in.

You can call on me, Nibra Ha Rishon, and ask me to channel the energies of the red ray to support you to maintain the vibration you have achieved. We will anchor this energy into your spinal column. Your spinal column, as you know, is a very important part of your body not just because it contains your interdimensional aspects but also because it is directly tied to your life force, which exists in the third chakra area. The third chakra and the spinal column are continuously interacting. Many energies go back and forth. Call on us, and we will anchor this energy into your spinal column. A lot of flushing and cleansing will naturally happen, and the fluid in the spinal column will be gently pushed up into your ascension chakra, which is in the back of your neck and also in your pineal gland and your right hemisphere.

We do this service because we see that there is a very high potential for you to continue the pace, to continue to be in the shift, and to maintain the vibration you achieved in 2012. We have noticed that many good people and many lightworkers kind of "lost it" after 2012. They had false beliefs about what 2012 actually was. They thought they would be beamed up, that life would be very different. But nothing changed. Their focus was only on the destination. When they came to the station, they were disappointed. Nothing happened. Their lives seemed tough again. They still had to pay their bills. They had no money in their pockets. Many have given up and are ready to go Home now, feeling deceived and fooled. Nothing seems to have shifted at all. Everything got worse after 2012.

Never Lose Hope

As you know, the real work started after 2012. You are now building your own railway tracks for the new consciousness. Your new train will run on these tracks, and you design the train as you did the tracks.

To lay and maintain the tracks and to run the engine, you need to know that this is a new journey. Be optimistic, have courage, and identify where we can support you. Maintaining the vibration you achieved in 2012, working with us, and keeping the same energy while slowly increasing it will propel you to new ideas, new thought forms, and new creations. Although you do not fully know how this will be done or where you are going, never lose hope.

You might say, "I do not know where I am going, but I must continue to build my tracks, for one day, my engine and train will run on these tracks." This is what explorers did when they set out on a journey. They did not know whether they would reach their destination or whether they would come back. They followed the stars, and they were often wrong, but they persevered. They kept their optimism, and that carried them forward.

I would like to repeat an old fable, the story of the frog in the milk pot. The frog saw the milk and he jumped into the pot to drink it, but then he started to drown. In desperation, he splashed in the milk with all of his little legs and became very tired. He just kept splashing, for there was nothing else he could do. He knew he was going to die, but he told himself, "I would rather die trying."

He kept beating the milk, and it eventually turned into butter. Then he jumped out of the milk pot.

There is a similar story of the donkey who fell into a ditch. Village people determined that it would be too difficult to get the donkey out of the ditch, so they tried to bury him alive. They dumped mud into the ditch. He shook his body so the mud did not stick. Slowly the mud rose high enough for him to jump out of the ditch.

We are doing the same thing. We are putting mud in your ditch. We are creating butter for you. On days when you feel completely lost or hopeless and nothing seems to work in your life, that thought alone will lower your vibration. Call on us.

We are a part of the first ray, and we love God from an angelic perspective. We anchor this energy into your spinal cord. Those of you who wish to avail yourselves of our services may contact us anytime in your meditation or quiet time. We will welcome you and work with you. I am Nibra Ha Rishon.

• • •

The Key to Your Next Life

This is Archangel Michael. I encourage you to work with this grand angel. It has been a challenge for humans to maintain their vibration, and many have lost hope and faith after 2012. Many want to go Home now, feeling they did the hard work and the heavy lifting, but nothing happened. The hardest part of building the road is going on right now. This angel and his council can support you. So I encourage you to call on the grand masters. Invoke this beautiful red color. This is Archangel Michael.

• • •

Hello. I am Lord Shiva. You might ask why Shiva comes in for a book on angels. Please remember, we are all part of the great process you call creation. I am one of the holy ghosts.

It is difficult to maintain your equilibrium, confidence, light, and vibration now. This is especially true when you leave your body. Your life flashes through your mind before you leave. This is a thought form you carry about what happened with each person in your life. Some people experience great sadness, defeat, rejection, and failure when they see what they did to others and what others did to them. This life review is deliberately set up for the time before you pass away. When you work with Nibra Ha Rishon and through the vibrational frequencies of light, he will anchor into your spinal column, and you will be able to erase a lot of the past.

During your last moment, past events you once feared do not seem as profound or severe as when they happened during your lifetime. Otherwise, you feel what you did to people and what they did to you, and you are not able to maintain your vibration. If it is just a fleeting memory passing through your thoughts, you will still be able to maintain your vibration. This is the key for your next life. You want to be reborn with a higher consciousness.

Call on this angel, Nibra Ha Rishon, and you will see dramatic changes happen. The past will not matter much. What happened twenty-five years ago will not matter because it will be a faded memory with no emotional charge. I support what Archangel Michael said. Work with this grand one to shift your life. This is Shiva.

• • •

Purify and Shift Your Vibration

Blessings, my name is Tahariel. I am the angel of purity. What does purity mean — purity in your life, in your soul, in your mind, in the vibration you hold? You can hold many different types of vibration. You are constantly creating different types of vibration and energy.

There are thought processes or emotional responses and reactions based on your belief systems. I work to bring purity to your vibration so that you can see how the vibrations inside you create a thought or an emotion, which creates a specific reality in reaction.

Have you ever wondered, "Is the vibration inside of me pure?" Have you thought of that? What's your answer?

Yes. It is not pure.

If you were to purify the vibration inside, the outer manifestation of everything in your life would naturally come from purity. My task, my duty, my job is to help people come to this level of understanding, for you are all energy, and you are all vibration. You are aware of this, but understanding vibrational purity is essential, because if your vibration is not sanctified, healed, or clarified, what is already there can build and perpetuate.

No matter how hard you try on the outside, if the vibration inside you is not pure, the energy created through your outer efforts (meditating, chanting, toning, or anything else) will not match. It must click with what is inside. People understand very little about this. They pray, they meditate, they chant, and they do affirmations, but there is not much effect. This is because the vibration inside of them is different. It is old, stagnant, outdated, and impure.

What is the vibration you carried, even as a child? Did the circumstances and conditions you experienced in the womb create a pure vibration? You could say that the womb keeps you pure and that you feel the love of the angels who are with you when you are born. What about the vibration you hold inside?

In America, and elsewhere, children as young as four or five behave violently. A five-year-old boy told a five-year-old girl he would shoot her.[1] This was in the news recently. How can a five-year-old boy come to know this? Psychologists might think he watched too much television or might blame his home environment. These are only triggers. What is the vibration carried by a ten-year-old boy who kills a ninety-year-old woman?[2] People come up with different theories. Psychologists and social workers will blame the parents or someone else. But they do not look at the vibration the child brought in at birth. Is it a hard vibration? Is it a vibration of destruction? You answer the question yourself.

If you call on us when a child is born and throughout childhood, we can constantly gauge the vibration of a child so that he or she only carries the purest vibration, and perhaps there will be a difference in the world. In addition, you can call on me to purify your vibration — to bring forth the vibration that matches your intention to find God within you and be the God you are in your everyday life. This is a new tool. I have never spoken to anyone of this. It is coming through Rae for the first time now. Very little is understood about this.

Energy and vibration are two different things. Some people think they are the same thing. We say no; they are different. Energy can be shifted more easily than vibration can be changed. Vibrations can be so stuck inside the deepest part of you that even if you try many things, like bringing higher-dimensional light, you are not able to maintain the energy because your vibration is stuck deep down at a lower level.

You often feel good during a meditation, but afterward, you are back to square one. You brought in energy, but you were not able to shift your vibration. Some of these vibrations can be like a chain around your ankles, your neck, or your shoulders. They often come from past lives, and of course, this life. But for many people, their basic vibration is coming from past lives.

---

1. In January, 2015, New Hampshire news reported that a kindergarten boy allegedly threatened to shoot a classmate. Read the story at http://www.wmur.com/news/parent-says-scholl-didn't-do-enough-after-boy-threatened-daughter/30684734.
2. In 2014, a Pennsylvania boy allegedly beat a ninety-year-old woman to death. Read the story at http://wnep.com/2014/13/10-year-old-boy-charged-with-homicide-of-90-year-old-woman/.

You must realize this: Energy converts into vibrational patterns. Energy is the raw material that creates the vibration. Say you want to make steel. Many raw materials go into steel — iron, carbon, whatever. Once steel is created, it becomes hard. It cannot be broken, but it can become brittle. This is similar to energy and vibration. Energy creates vibrational patterns, and then it becomes stuck inside of you.

Call on me to come with a gift. I am a coil made of many metals, including copper. Ask me to place this coil on you, and I will connect with your vibrational energy and suck out all the energy that is not pure. When this happens, there will be a loosening of energy. This transforms your vibration into something else, sometimes even back into its original form. Alchemy happens. Your vibration is transformed into something else. Ask for this instrument, this coil, and the purity coil of Angel Tahariel.

How often would we do this? Would this be a daily exercise to do for a while?

Initially you should work with this for a while, for there is much to be changed. Imagine a beautiful light coming into you as I place this coil of light into your vibrational body. Did you know that each human being carries a vibrational body? It is not just the energetic body but also the vibrational body. When you bring in light, also bring it into your vibrational body, because true change must happen in your vibration, not just in your energy. Energy creates vibration. Energy is like the vegetables, spices, and the other ingredients. Vibration is the food cooked. You can and must change your vibration now. It comes from your ancient past.

You will see a great change in humanity. You may wonder about the radicalism you see today, how young people can become so radicalized. They came from good families and had good upbringings, but what changed? Look into their vibration.

Heal Vibrational Patterns

In the future, there will be healing for vibrational patterns. What are vibrational patterns? When the vibration becomes increasingly polluted, this creates different geometric patterns that are not in harmony with the original geometric patterns of the body. In a way, there is a tug of war going on. It is similar to cancer; it fights with the beautiful healthy cells.

You can also call the deva (or deity) of your vibration, for you have a goddess working with the vibrational pattern inside you. Call on this being. You can also call on me, for I am the great purifier, Angel Tahariel.

• • •

This is Archangel Michael. Any questions?

Would it be better to take an extended period of time to purify my vibration, like a whole day or a weekend, or is it better to practice it daily?

This depends on what you want to change. Initially, you can call on Angel Tahariel in your meditations. Ask him to come into your presence and restore and purify your vibration. You will feel some electrical currents or shifting of energy. That is how you know it is working. You will feel a sense of lightness, a sense of brightness, and a sense of more divinity or sacredness within yourself. There will be a repatterning of your cells — changing the information in your cells, your bones, and your blood. A reconfiguration can happen. You are shifting, and sometimes that can be disorienting, but it will pass quickly.

This is one of the reasons why many people are stubborn. They think they are not stubborn. They try, but they cannot change because their vibration is stuck in one pattern. Without the vibration shifting and changing, energy cannot truly be shifted.

We are bringing radical teachings, for we want people to think outside of the box, take a fresh look at their lives. Are they happy people? Of course not. So they need radical thinking and radical teaching.

Changing Your Vibration Is Quicker Than Energy Work

As we change our vibration, will this affect our health? Disease seems to come from holding on to the wrong vibration. Is that correct?

Exactly. Wrong thoughts, wrong beliefs, and wrong ideas about yourself can all cause disease. Let us say you do not really love yourself, and these thoughts convert into energy and become your vibrational pattern. This can create disoriented geometric patterns, which can cause problems in your body. Do you want to change? If your vibration changes, there will be a release, a shift, and a possibility of being healed.

But where does this vibrational pattern start from? It goes very deep. This is why we suggested that you work with the Karmic Board, for it has the capacity to help. It is a support system made up of the angels and others to shift your vibrational patterns.[3]

Let me give you an example. After the great tragedy of 9/11, the people of

3. See *DNA of the Spirit, Vol. 1*, page 195 and chapter 4 of this book for discussions on working with Karmic Board.

your country hardened their hearts through their thinking, actions, and beliefs. They closed their hearts out of fear and paranoia and created a very specific vibrational pattern. This pattern became stuck in the collective consciousness. Many actions are now coming from that vibrational pattern. Is this healthy? Is this supporting humanity? You can answer those questions yourself. The same is true for Israel. Like human beings, countries also have vibrations that can get stuck, and what these countries do comes from this stuck vibration.

People do not realize what is happening. Many people try to change themselves with energy work, but not much happens. Shamans try to change the energy of a country, but nothing much changes. They must go into the vibration of the country, which has already hardened. They must work from there.

This is the true meaning of the saying, "Life is an effect, not the cause." The cause was an incident where energy was created, and with that energy, a vibration was created. If you change that vibration, you will change the present vibration within your being.

How can we change a country's vibration, such as the fear and paranoia in the United States caused by 9/11?

This requires collective work. This is why we are bringing this understanding of vibration. We ask you to work with Tahariel, the angel of purity, to learn how you can shift the vibration of anything.

If we start with ourselves, maybe once we get the hang of it, then we can start working on a larger level.

Larger levels will come with time. For example, the vibrational patterns of much of the fruit and vegetables you eat have been manipulated. Once you have an understanding of vibrations, then you can say, "I need to shift the vibration of this pineapple (or this banana)." True change will come from vibrational shifting rather than from energetic work. Energy work will still work, but it will take a much longer time and the constant downloading of higher energy, which many people are not able to do. Go into vibrations, like we said, and you will be able to shift it.

Is this similar to going to the Karmic Board for help?

It is all interrelated.

So we don't necessarily have to identify the reasons we have impure vibrations. We can just ask for the vibration to be changed. Is that correct?

Yes, you can ask that your vibration be purified to its original source once per day. This is why we said that angels can play a much bigger role than people are aware of. This is why we want to bring understanding that working with angels can truly transform. These are new ideas we are bringing forth at this time.

Healers Can Call on Tahariel

When I am doing energy work on someone, would it be appropriate for me to ask Angel Tahariel to come forward and purify this person to his or her original vibration?

You may call for this angel. Yes, of course, but one must be a willing participant to work with this angel. Tahariel can support you, but your clients must also fully participate and ask for their vibrations to be restored. This is cooperation between you and the angel. Yes, it can be done. First, you must work on yourself to determine how you feel about it. It is definitely possible.

Most people I work with have strong intentions to make changes. That's why they are there. But sometimes I think the work I am doing is of limited effectiveness.

When you are trying to work with vibrations, you will see quantum shifts. Look at your own life. Which areas feel stuck? Ask whether your vibration is stuck there. You can use divining rods to help you. In any important area of your life, first ask whether your energy is okay for that area. Then ask whether the vibrational pattern of this energy is good. Is it stuck, or is it flowing with you? Then you can ask to shift it. Ask if once you shift your vibration, whether you are able to shift the energy within you. Then ask whether working with this angel in this process can be supported.

Then work with that. This is the truth. The energy of Angel Tahariel is very pure and very soft. You will be uplifted.

• • •

How to Maintain the Vibration of Love

This is the Violet Angel. Blessings and love to you all. I have come to speak about love. Love is a vibration. It is not a feeling or an emotion. I am connected with emotions and feelings. But this vibration can be raised or upgraded by your mind. The challenge is how to maintain love constantly, growing with it.

Imagine that you are an incubator with a beautiful egg inside of you. When you connect with me, I will send energy into the egg you carry. See yourself bursting out of the egg, bringing an incredible purple color. You are still in the incubator. You are a small baby. Lightworkers are putting beautiful purple light near you, and this violet color spreads throughout your being.

Your umbilical cord is still attached. The violet color goes through the umbilical cord, and like a fountain, it spews this color into your auric body and your other bodies. See the umbilical cord slowly shrinking in size and settling into your navel. The violet light will still be in the umbilical cord and your naval area for the next three days. Through the power of intention and meditation, see the umbilical cord open again and spew these beautiful colors.

You will feel a different vibration within you slowly emerging. You cannot describe this vibration; you can only experience it. You might feel good. You might feel alive, joyful, and buoyant. Anytime you feel sad, go into the incubator and send this vibration and color through the umbilical cord. The energy is still there. Do it for one to three minutes, and you will feel a shift. You can do it anytime you choose.

I am the Angel of Violet.

• • •

Open the Golden Heart and Activate the Torus

Hello, family. You can just call me Lily Angel. I am the Angel of Flowers. You have heard that there are devas in flowers. We are like children. We carry pure vibrations and beauty like small children who know their inner worth. We know our inner worth and our beauty throughout our lifetimes. Even when we are dying and getting ready for the next cycle of our incarnation, we still know that

we are beautiful. We still know that we have completed a life cycle and that we are going to be reprocessed so that we can return again and be the beauty we are.

The Creator, in infinite wisdom, did not create flowers just for flowers. Flowers have meaning. You can call on us, the flower angels, to come and visit your house daily, even if you do not have flowers. Ask us to bring the energy of flowers and anchor this throughout your house. When you start doing this, you will start appreciating yourself more and value yourself.

We have seen that human beings have little value for themselves. They might say they value themselves — yes, to a certain degree, this is true — but they do not 100 percent. Invite us and make us a part of you, a guest staying in your house. You will begin to remember a little bit more of yourself, and you will love yourself more. We have the capacity to open hearts in more ways than people realize. Why do you think we are in weddings, a gift when you date, or when you have a birthday? Why do you need flowers? Flowers further open your heart, for we have this capacity.

You each have a heart consciousness called the golden heart. In addition to the heart chambers you are aware of, there is also one called the golden heart. Invite us, and we will work with you in opening your golden heart. This golden heart is four-sided and directly connected to the four directions — east, west, south, and north. When you open your golden heart, you are coming from a higher space. You will create a higher reality.

Many of you want to work with the energy of the torus but find it difficult to do so. When you activate your torus, this energy must go through your golden heart and through the four directions. Only then will you be able to feel the energy. By the way, do you know that the four directions are directly related to your internal compass? The four directions affect human beings emotionally and intuitively.

Some ancient cultures, like those in China, knew about this. They call it feng shui, but they do not go into its deeper aspects. This affects your heart. You can call on us to open the four-directional heartbeat, the golden heart. You will experience an immediate uplifting of your energy, your perception, and an understanding of this larger truth that you can tap into. Would you invite me, the great Lily Angel, to your house? I am pretty. I am beautiful. I extend my invitation to all of you.

• • •

This is Archangel Michael. When you open the golden heart of the four

directions, you will see your life expand in every way. You will feel much expansive energy coming into you. The directions were created not because you had to go from place to place. There is a greater purpose. They are your supporting energies, just like plants support you. There are east angels, west angels, south angels, and north angels. Everything is designed with perfection and with a master plan. Look into that.

Call for the golden heart of the four directions. You know about the great teaching called the *I Ching*. This came about when Master Lao Tzu[4] opened the golden heart of the four directions. This teaching is an ancient form of divination.

You are familiar with the Flower of Life. The Flower of Life is directly connected to the four directions and the golden heart. That is why it has stood the test of time. When people see the Flower of Life, it speaks to them on some level, for it represents the four hearts. We are so joyful and thankful to be able to bring this understanding to humanity.

You will see more and more teachings coming to enlighten and truly support people. Many new teachings will come not only through Rae but also from others around the world. You have an expression, "When the student is ready, the teacher appears." This is happening now. If humanity is ready, we are all ready. Rae is ready. That is why we are coming through at this time. It is a beautiful

4. Loa Tzu is known as the father of Taoism. Learn more about him at http://www.chebucto.ns.ca/Philosophy/Taichi/lao.html.

partnership. It is the true meaning of partnering with angels. You will have very interesting angels speaking with you in the future.

We are pleased and overjoyed because when this transmission goes on, many beings are here. They hear what is coming through, and they applaud all of you. During this transmission, more than fifty beings of light were here.

Blessings. This is Archangel Michael.

• • •

Experience the Buddha Within

Hello, once again. This is Archangel Metatron with the angelic beings of light. We would like to share a message from Master Buddha that can help you transform your thinking and your perception of reality.

Close your eyes, and breathe three or four times. Say, "I give intention to experience the energy of the Buddha within me." Open your eyes after about thirty seconds.

How do you feel?

Speaker 1: I feel an animated peacefulness and deep self-worth.
Speaker 2: I feel very peaceful, and it has been a hectic day, so the peace feels very good.
Speaker 3: I feel my heart opening up, and I feel great compassion for everyone.
Speaker 4: I feel energized.

What does this exercise do? What was Buddha trying to teach people? It is simple. All the energy that you seek is already inside you. That means there is no separation between you and Buddha. You are a group energy, and one of the energies you carry is the energy of Master Buddha. I will give another exercise for you to do.

Close your eyes once again, and breathe. Breathe deeply. Bring a great whale to your mind's eye. This can be any kind of whale. Say, "I give intention to experience the energy of this magnificent lightbeing, this whale within me now." Just breathe it in, only a few more seconds. You can open your eyes.

How do you all feel now, dear ones?

Speaker 4: I have a fabulous feeling all over.
Speaker 3: I feel lifted out of my personality into something much more universal and very impersonal and beautiful. It is great. It is hard to describe it.
Speaker 2: I feel a very deep warmth in the center of my being radiating out.
Speaker 1: I feel a great expansion of consciousness. I think what Robert said was accurate. It feels like being lifted into another form of feeling and a great wisdom.

You have just broken a great barrier in your lives. Imagine being able to feel everything, even a tree. The great tree spirit is inside of you, the spirit of a bird is within you, and the spirit of a lotus flower is in you. You will slowly start breaking the walls of separation consciousness, and then you will see, "I Am That I Am. I am the lotus. I am the whale. I am the Buddha." It is very simple. But if you were to sit with the Buddha's energy or the energy of a whale for a few minutes, you would be so uplifted. You would open up to those parts inside you that will further enlighten you.

Tomorrow when you wake up, you can say, "I give the intention to experience the energy of (pick one thing, pick anything) within me." You are all advanced students. You can ask, "I give intention to experience the energy of the stars, the planets." Can you imagine what would happen? What happened today? You would be in a very high place.

You incorporate that consciousness into your consciousness?

You do not incorporate it. It is already there. You open it, and activate it. You give intention to experience it.

Being one with everything.

Exactly. I want you to work with it.

Slowly you will come to realize that there has never been a separation. When you come to this place, your vibration will shoot up, and slowly you will come into the place of communion with all. Play with it, dear ones. It is great fun. Experience the energy of the rose within you. Experience the energy of the dandelion, the wind, the Sun, or the energy of the planet Venus within you. A simple exercise done every day can have a profound effect. Work with this every day or two.

Experience the Sound Vibration of Your Soul Name

I would like to show you one more exercise.

Close your eyes, breathe, and say, "I give intent to experience the energy of the holy and sacred sound within me now." It is the energy of the holy and sacred sound within you. Just breathe it in.

You can open your eyes now. How do you feel?

Speaker 1: I feel like the origins of Om.

Speaker 2: I got a kind of "ooh-ah" sound with a kind of humming vibration.

Speaker 3: As I began, I thought I would never be able to feel this, and then I started to feel something, but I can't describe it. It just felt good.
Speaker 4: The Om came through to me very strongly.
Speaker 5: Beautifully elevated.

If you want to experiment, you can state, "I give intent to experience the sound vibration of my soul name within me." When you are at that level, when you are able to connect with that energy, you will feel it right away. These are life-changing shifts. Simple exercises can change a lot.

One thing to realize is many will not accept even this simple truth, and many will not feel it because their belief systems do not support it. But you are already graduate students.

Blessings, and I am with all of you. This is Archangel Metatron.

Thank you very much.

• • •

Awaken the Adam Kadmon Energy Within

Hello, brothers of light and sisters of love. My name is Tadzekiel. I am the archangel who puts things together to show you the way to connect, embrace, experience, and integrate the energy of your Adam Kadmon.

You have gathered all the wisdom of your lifetimes, including what you learned in these sessions. It must all be put into perspective and stitched together so that this energy can be focused for one purpose: your awakening, understanding, and enlightenment. I am the angel who stitches together the energy of the Adam Kadmon within you. Call on me in the early mornings and early evenings, for these are the best times for accessing high-vibrational energies.

Does this mean that other times are not good? I will not say that. I would say mornings and evenings are the best times in terms of energetic configurations. Your body undergoes changes in the mornings and evenings with the rising and setting of the Sun. There is a dynamic energy change in the physical body at this time.

These are special times — windows of opportunity. This was common practice for the people of ancient Asia. Their favorite and most powerful prayers were done at these times. There is a window. Call on me to stitch the energetic code of Adam Kadmon into you, for I will place the mantle of Adam Kadmon onto you and stitch it into your energetic bodies, combining all together, so that you may work in the fifth-dimensional reality at all times, not only when you are in a high state of consciousness during your meditation. I invite you into the magical world of Adam Kadmon, where true oneness can be experienced.

Very few have been able to achieve this on a constant and continuous basis, even after ascension. After you ascend, you experience a new reality on the Earth plane. It takes a long time for the full energy of ascension to be integrated for you to be able to live in it continuously. One of the grand masters who did so was the master called Lahiri Mahasaya from ancient India. He was a teacher of the master Sri Yukteswar, who was the teacher of Paramahansa Yogananda [author of *Autobiography of a Yogi*]. Lahiri Mahasaya was able to live continuously in an ascended state while still living and performing everyday tasks, including being a husband. I offer the same gift to all of you at this time.

The Adam Kadmon Key

Did I hear correctly that you are an archangel?

Yes. Are there any questions?

You said you were the energy of Adam Kadmon.

No, I stitch the energy of the Adam Kadmon into you. I am the key to integrating and anchoring all the energies of Adam Kadmon fully into you, to stitch them into your reality so that you can experience Adam Kadmon.

So you are the key.

Exactly, yes, I am the key.

Can you explain to me what Adam Kadmon is?

Adam Kadmon simply means God-human, the first Adam created by God in the perfect and fullest expression of God.

Close your eyes. Place your hands on your hearts, and say, "I call on Archangel Tadzekiel, and I give intent to experience the energy of Adam Kadmon within me, right now. It may be a flicker, but I can make it into a raging fire so that it becomes a permanent part of me, because I am able to feel it." Say, "I give intent to experience the Adam Kadmon within me now."

There will be a vibration; there will be a feeling. How do you all feel, brothers and sisters of light?

Pretty amazing. I could feel it immediately. I felt shooting energy up and down my spine, all the way down to my feet and up to the back of my head.

You are right on target. How do you feel, sister?

I feel the same thing. The energy is all connected, and I feel alive.

Exactly. Very true, and how do you feel, sister?

Very vibrant.

Yes, how do you feel, brother?

Yes, it is the essence from the tree of life.

Exactly. You got it right — the essence of the tree of life. And how do you feel, sister?

I feel energy going up through my feet.

Exactly. This energy exists, but it is very flickering. With my help, it can become a raging fire within you. Are you ready to experience awesome power within you?

We are offering this incredible gift to all of you at this time. I will fully awaken this Adam Kadmon energy and stitch it into the core of you, and it will become a part of you every moment in everyday reality. I work with your full I Am presence and your council of guides. You will be given only that which you are able to handle. In the first two to three months, you will feel an increase in vibration of between 30 to 40 percent. Just imagine what you could do with 40 percent more energy. This is my gift to all of you.

Christine has just had a profound experience, and she is in tears, so she could probably use a little stabilizing energy right now.
It is like the universe is opening up within me.

This is good, sister. This is what we said.

It is very, very good.

Dear one, you are touching the Divine within you. We are offering this experience of the Divine to you. You can touch it, not just in this moment. It becomes a part of you. You will be able to feel the 30 to 40 percent increase in three months. Imagine what your life will become! Call on me, Archangel Tadzekiel, and we will work with you, because when this happens, the universe rejoices. Everybody on this side knows another one has awakened fully. Others can see this light from our side. I will give you a mantra, Sister Christine, so that you may never forget yourself again, from now onward.

[Chants:] Tariie. I am Tariie, a sister of light, a fully awakened sister of light. I am Tariie. I am the star, the awakened one.

Good day to all of you.

Thank you.

• • •

This is Archangel Michael. Are you all enjoying today's session, dear ones?

Christine has dissolved into a puddle of tears.

When you know yourself, you cry. But you have incredible power. We ask you to come to this place of no separation.

• • •

This is Metatron. It is time to work so that you will be able to experience more of yourself. When you say, "I give intention to experience the energy of Adam Kadmon within me," you will see a massive shift in your consciousness — a greater perception and an opening in your reality. When you make this intention, it opens a portal inside your pineal and pituitary glands that make it easy to tap into higher realities.

When you do this, you are not spaced-out. You are grounded and very well balanced.

• • •

Ground Yourself with Dragon Energy and Dragon Codes

Hello, blessed ones. My name is Suria. I am one of the angels who supports Mother Earth. Mother Earth has many supporting energies. I am one of the angels who supports one of her supporting energies, the energy of dragons. Dragons are vitally important for Mother Earth. So are dolphins and whales. Dolphins carry much earth energy within their beings, and through this, they emit earth energy to people.

There is a council of dragons, and there are dragon beings who meditate on sending grounding earth energy into the beings throughout the world. When you are grounded, then you are in a better state of mind. You can make better choices.

Dragons send benevolent, balanced energies. Just imagine if all the people in the world were well grounded. Do you think there would be conflict? Perhaps none or very little. Minds would be clearer. There would be less fear. If you are grounded, even when someone insults you or throws a temper tantrum, there is a high likelihood that you would not react. You might respond after consideration, but you would not react right away because you are grounded.

Dragons send this energy to people every day. This has been going on for thousands of years. We need to send our deepest appreciation and love to the dragons for doing this, for animals hold the vibration for the planet. If there were no animals, you would not live long. You would all die quite young, at thirty-five to forty-five years of age. I, along with others, support the beings who support Mother Earth.

Since you are part of Mother Earth's body, it is only natural that we also work with you, if called on, so that you can become grounded and balanced. We travel throughout this planet anchoring this energy. There is much supporting energy around the planet. Otherwise, the world would have already taken another direction.

There are old stories about Atlas[5] holding the globe on his head. We (along with others) hold specific vibrations on our heads so that Earth is stable. You can call on us every day so that you become grounded and balanced — a being of response, not reaction.

There is dragon energy inside every human being. It is a supporting energy that you can bring forth, but it must be activated within you. Dragon energies are powerful. They exist in certain areas of your body. They exist in the back of your body, in the back of your neck, and in the palms and tips of your fingers. You can activate this energy within you, and it will support you.

You can ask the dragon codes to be activated within you. Dragon code energies are very strong. One must be able to handle these energies benevolently. Ask for guidance and protection before you do this. You do not want to do this too quickly. You want to be balanced while holding this vibration.

Blessings. I am the angel who supports the energies of Mother Earth. Our work is about the power within you — the force within you, the vastness within you, the strength within you, and the God power within you, fully realized.

5. Atlas was given the task of holding the heavens on his shoulders as punishment from Zeus for leading the Titans in the battle to control the heavens. For more information, see http://www.ancient.eu/Atlas.

CHAPTER SIX

Practice Universal Communication

Angel Raffa, Angel Anauel, Angel Aramm, Archangel Michael, Angel Agon, Angel Ebed, Angel Haaiaha

Hello, my dear friends. My name is Raffa. What I can do for you is very simple. By calling and connecting with my name, my energy, and my vibration, I will teach you to distinguish whether the thoughts coming into your mind are from your soul or elsewhere. I taught Master Jesus how to distinguish whether it was his soul or his mind speaking from a past experience or from the matrix. It is absolutely critical to realize and distinguish your inner voice.

Learn to Decipher the Voice of Your Soul

In this fast-paced time of spiritual growth and evolution, so much is being given through various media, mediums, and channels, not all of which are of the light or of the highest vibration of truth. Some of them are picking up a different reality and bringing it forth. This has an affect. When you read this material, it affects you because you give power to what you read, whether it is of a loving nature or not.

You can develop the ability to distinguish whether something is coming from Source or elsewhere. I have rarely spoken to human beings, but I now feel it is time for humanity to connect. This is a critical factor as you move into the next level — and the next level and the next level. Your soul will whisper more and more, but often simultaneous voices will start whispering louder and louder. These simultaneous voices are the voices of your personality, your mental body, your emotional body, or your physical body. Since you have had so many experiences in past lives, the voices of these other bodies are much stronger, more vibrant, and more present than the whispers of your soul, which is always subtle.

You often say, "This is my soul whispering. I know it is." But often it is not. The other voices are stronger. If this is not controlled, it can have devastating effects on your spiritual growth. You must constantly ask whether even this truth — what I am now speaking or anything you read or hear — comes from your soul or elsewhere.

It is truly difficult to control your thoughts. It is said simply that you cannot control your thoughts, but you can control thoughts that keep you where you are. This is not easy. The energy imprints of past experiences and behaviors, your patterns — not only of the physical body, but also other bodies — embed and become your reality. What you believe, you will create, and you think that this is your reality. Often this is not from your soul. I ask you to call on me, and we will work with color spectrums to remove these energetic imprints so that we can imprint new vibrations of thought patterns.

There is an energy inside of you that is very alive. You can also call on this being to work along with me. This being is called the thought adjuster. Many beings live inside your physical body. You can call on the thought adjuster to shift the frequencies of patterned energy imprints coming from all your other bodies. This is very important at this time.

There are nerve centers that come down from the head, go through the back of your neck, and go into the back of your body. They create certain patterns of thought when you experience something in your outer reality. It is a predetermined action, response, or reaction. You need to clear this. These patterns were established not only in this lifetime but also go back 30,000 to 40,000 years.

Receive the Energy of Your Soul

You have heard of the fight-or-flight syndrome? It is embedded in the back of your body through your nervous system. Your nervous system carries tremendous energy and past memories. When you run a specific color combination through these nerves, it can remove old patterning. I work with the spectrum of colors, and there are energetic configurations in the brain that can change the energy and the patterns of how you think.

There are energies in your toes that have important implications about how you live your life, whether you are living from your highest level or from a fight-or-flight mentality. These energetic imprints must be removed. They are in the soles of your feet and are embedded deeply inside your toes.

Imagine you are wearing colorful sandals; they have as many colors as you can imagine. See your feet becoming full of colors. Your feet pulse with a mixture of colors, and then they disperse light. This removes plaque attached to the bones on your soles. The pulsing colors cleanse and remove energy. See these colors slowly moving up through your hips, into your back, and into your spinal column. The predominant colors are fall colors — soft maroon, beige, and light green becoming light yellow. But there is a metallic tone to these colors, and they slowly move up through your head. Now your head is filled with these incredible colors, and they have the potential to remove old patterning from all your bodies.

Work constantly with this for the next several days until it becomes very clear that what you hear is the voice of truth from your own soul, especially in relation to spiritual matters. You cannot give up your mind. You need your mind to carry out the tasks set forth by your soul.

People say, "I do not hear my soul. I have tried many times. I communicate. I do everything." Are they truly able to hear and discern what their souls are saying? Perhaps not. Work with me for the next twenty-one days to prepare yourself to be able to receive the energy of your soul more fully. You might move fully into the new reality in which you will be able to hear more clearly.

When you start hearing your thoughts, it's almost as if they each have a personality. Is that what you mean, you can recognize whether a person is positive or negative?

I would not say it is positive or negative. What we are trying to say is how you can best hear your soul rather than thoughts originating from your mental, emotional, or physical body. This is critical, because the more the soul comes into you, the more integration happens. Your soul is going to speak more and more, but your soul always speaks with the softest of voices.

We have found that many lightworkers are not fully able to distinguish between their souls' thoughts and their minds' thoughts. They say, "I have seen the signs. I prayed and did other things." This could be true, but you often create these through projections. You create the sign through your intention, but it might not be fully from your soul.

Brother Kryon mentioned this: If you had many lives doing one particular thing, you would come back to this life wanting to do that same thing. You would feel restless and seek a calling in your heart.

We paraphrase a story told by Brother Kryon (a wonderful angel) about a little boy who wanted to be a fisherman when he was growing up.[1] He used to go to the seashore whenever he found the time. He started talking to fishermen,

1. Lee Carroll, *The Parables of Kryon* (Carlsbad, California: Hay House Books, 2001) pp. 119–120.

and he could talk to them as if he were one of them. He told his parents he was going to become a fisherman. He could tie nets with them, just like a fisherman. But his father thought that this was not a good idea, so he put his son in a college far away.

The son graduated, became a lawyer, got married, and settled down. People said, "Why not become the mayor?" Reluctantly, he agreed, and they elected him mayor. As mayor, he was able to bring forth understanding, decisions, and choices that affected millions of people. Because he had been a fisherman in so many lifetimes, he had a good understanding of how to communicate, bargain, and heal rifts between two parties. The soul takes the wisdom from the many past lives and uses it for a higher good. Since he had been a fisherman, he wanted to be a fisherman. But is that your soul's agenda for you, or is something else? This is the key.

Brother Kryon teaches that the soul takes wisdom from the past to create a grand reality. Since you have had so many lifetimes doing the same thing, you feel very pulled to do the same thing again, but that may not be what your soul chooses for you to experience now. This definitely happens for lightworkers.

Work with us, and we will bring forth understanding. We will remove energetic imprints from the past not just from the physical body but also from the mental and emotional bodies, so a new pathway can be created, and you will be able to hear more of your soul.

Work with Color to Connect with the Soul

Could you summarize what you suggest we do for the next twenty-one days to work with you in order to establish this connection with the soul?

Work with color: *Imagine and visualize that you are wearing color sandals that are emitting all colors of light, especially metallic fall colors. The colors go through your soles and remove the plaque embedded in your toes. This is where the fight-or-flight syndrome originates. Then take these pulsing colors to your hips and run them through your spinal column, pushing them through the neck all the way to the middle of your head.*

How do we monitor ourselves to see whether we are doing these exercises properly? When I ask for your support, how will I know that I am actually feeling your vibration?

Follow your feelings. When you follow your feelings, you are the judge, and you will know. It is a feeling and a sense of knowing. Although you may not see anybody, you might sense the energy and feel the warmth, vibration, love, and expansion. That is all that is required.

We would like you to change your focus when you ask to integrate your consciousness with someone you are asking for help. Form the intention of experiencing and connecting with the energy you already have inside you. For example, "I give intention to connect with the energy of Angel Raffa, which is already inside of me." When you ask in this way, there is no separation in consciousness.

When you shift to this focus, a shift in consciousness can happen rapidly, and the gap will no longer be there. You will realize that what you have been looking for has always existed within you. When this shift happens, you will immediately exclaim, "I got it! My God! After so many times, I just got it!" Do you understand what I am trying to say?

Yes. Do not seek from outside but rather from within ourselves.

Make the intention to experience what you already have inside of you. You can form the intention of experiencing the energy of the Adam code[2] or the multiuniversal energy within you. Then you will be coming from a very high place. You will see a shift right away. You will start to see that you are one with everything, and there is no separation. You have heard about this many times, but a sudden realization will come; a sense of knowingness and beingness happens, and with that, a major shift takes place. True communion happens, and the illusion of the separation slowly starts to fade. It still exists, but you also know that it is only an illusion. You are much more aware and conscious of it as such.

Let us say you intend to connect with the energy of Master Thoth, which is a part of you; the energy of the Great Pyramid, which is part of you; or the energy of Mary Magdalene, which is part of you. There is instant connection, for they are always there.

• • •

Alter the Energy of Business

Hello, my friend, my name is Anauel. I support commerce and business. Commerce and business, trading with a fair exchange of energy, are very important. This is a healthy part of every culture. In older times, it was done through an exchange of services [barter], and now this is slowly returning. This is the energy of exchange between two people: one who has something to sell and one who needs what the other has.

2. Rae Chandran with Robert Mason Pollack, *DNA of the Spirit, Volume 2* (Flagstaff, Arizona: Light Technology Publishing, 2014) chapter 6.

In many ways, the intention behind the energy exchange has been lost. There is imbalance without equilibrium. In true commerce, the seller is satisfied with the sale he has made and the buyer is satisfied with what he receives. When both feel appreciated, they feel joyful, and a beautiful energy exchange happens. We can be called on to create an energy exchange in business in which both seller and consumer feel joyful. They will both feel as if they received fair deals.

Commerce is not just about introducing new products to gain market share. It is really about partnership and understanding that the energy of God is in everything. Business and commerce need to be looked at very differently. When you call on us, we can infuse you with new ideas, new thought forms, and new energy imprints about how you can conduct your business differently and still do well so that both parties feel good.

If you look at most businesses, the sellers might feel happy because they are able to sell a large quantity of products, but the buyers do not feel joyous, and there is nothing they can do. The buyers need the product sold by the sellers, so they have to buy it. Sellers often create incredible unhappiness and karma. Many companies do this. They do not realize they are creating great karma.

We support commerce that is done fairly — a fair distribution of products and a fair amount of energy received for the services offered. We have some mathematical equations that can be applied to any kind of commerce. This is how highly advanced societies work. Say we have a product we want to sell. Calculate the cost of the materials, production, and labor, as well as all the other costs like rent, taxes, and shipping. Add up all the costs and add another 20 percent for profit (incentive to invest in the business and have some savings for a rainy day). I am just giving you a ballpark figure; it could be 20 percent or 30 percent. Once this is established, the consumers know they will be paying a fair price. Sellers will feel they received a good value, and buyers will feel they have paid a fair price.

Business is now conducted very differently. Sellers often believe they took risks, so they charge 200 percent or even 500 percent over cost for profit. This is not equilibrium. This is greed.

There is a restaurant in America that follows a particular scheme.[3] Customers pay as much as they want; they determine the price. This restaurant found that 80 to 90 percent of their customers paid more than they would have if they had ordered from a priced menu. There will always be a few people who will

3. Pay-What-You-Can restaurant example: http://en.wikipedia.org/wiki/One_World_Cafe.

abuse the trust, but most people will feel good. They are honest and want to support this business.

You can call on us every day to bring you creative ideas. We can also remove unwanted energy. Many people in business are afraid of competition, so they use manipulative, deceptive tactics. They attract these kinds of energies.

When you encounter negative, difficult people, we will protect you, and you will find peace. We will also bring forth understanding of new ways of doing things, new inventions, and new ideas within the existing model of what you are doing. We have this capacity.

Here is a hypothetical example of fair commerce: A shoe company makes sneakers. This brand may cost $80 to $100 and is made in the Philippines or Indonesia, where the workers are paid $1 a day. (In many countries, the typical salary is only $40 or $50 a month.)

They can't afford to buy what they make.

Suppose this company raises its wages to $12 a day. In twenty-five days, the employees would earn $300. What would happen, dear one? They would increase their market.

The employees could become consumers.

Exactly! Eighty percent of the world population earns very little. Imagine what could happen to all the businesses. It would be a win-win for everyone. The corporation would have new customers, and the employees would be newly empowered beings.

It is very true, but so much of the business culture is about competition. I am totally for what you are suggesting here, but it seems that someone would look at that as an opportunity to sell for lower prices. There is so much competition in business. It is very cutthroat.

This is why we are trying to bring a different consciousness to all areas of life by partnering with angels. Some businesses could start doing things differently. Partnering with angels is not for everyone. But people who truly want to make a change and be more useful will start looking into this.

I am getting the picture that people who follow these new procedures would generate consciousness that is more positive and manifest abundance through their own actions.

Also less karma, so everyone wins.

Whereas some corporations that do things the old way are just adding to their karma, businesses following these new practices will generate a more positive consciousness and energy, so they would prosper.

They will manifest goodwill and good karma for the ground too. This fair exchange is called fair commerce. A time will come in the future when people will use the term "fair commerce"; not right now, but in forty to fifty years, this will be called fair commerce.

Is this the time to begin this?

Everything has a new beginning. In this moment, we have to do things in a new way. It might start with one person, one shop, one group; it has taken root. It can spread. It can spread from one company to another. The word gets around. This idea, once adopted, could be posted on the Internet and revolutionize the way people do things.

Even now, you see news stories in America about people starting companies in their homes or college dormitories, and then they sell their companies to a bigger company for sums like $100 million. The person who started the business takes care of all the employees who built the business. This is what we are talking about; everyone wins. We have created such good. This is one aspect of what we are talking about.

Once we start working with people who call on us, we will be able to bring forth new ideas, and they will be able to start doing things in a completely new way. You can also ask us for help to enhance your existing business without fear. Most people have fear. So much is based on fear. The winner takes all. Who is going to win the race?

I can see this happening with people who are willing to change their old paradigms. So much of what people learn about business is from business schools, where there is so much emphasis on competition and cost consciousness. Labor is not about a human being; rather, it is seen as an expense. All that will change.

Has this made the world better?

No, it hasn't at all. It is terrible. It's a madhouse.

You must ask whether things are working. Maybe it is time to look at doing things differently.

You don't need to talk me into it! No, I'm totally on board with that. It just takes people to start it, and then the snowball starts to grow.

Exactly. And people will accept these ideas. They will see. It is time to look at doing things differently.

This is Anauel.

• • •

The Sky Can Help You Remember Why You Are Here

My name is Angel Aramm. I am the Angel of the Sky. Although the sky may look the same, if you really observe, you will see different patterns, different colors, and different energies in different countries and in different directions. The sky may look the same to you in North Africa as in Japan. But if you were to really observe it, you would see slight differences. Differences exist.

The sky is an integral part of your life. How is this so? The sky projects to the people living in every land, reminding them of the karmic energy they have come with and the lessons they need to complete lest they forget. People living in Africa have different karma and different lessons from the people living in Japan. This is why there are differences in the colors, shades, and vibrations of the sky, for the energy beamed to each person is different. The sky helps them. It reminds people why they are here, what their life lessons are, and what they have come here to achieve.

The sky works with the water element in your physical body, which contains your blueprint. Why you are here is embedded in the water molecules of your body. When a baby is in the mother's womb, the baby's guides pass this information to the mother energetically. As the child grows up in a third-dimensional world, he or she naturally forgets the blueprint. But if you were to connect with the sky and ask for the downloading of the lessons you have come here to learn, you will have increased remembrance of why you are here.

Here is an exercise for you to work with. Go outside and look at the clouds. Blow into the clouds three times, and say, "Please move." You will see the clouds move. How can your gentle blowing reach the sky, which is so far away? There are beings in the clouds who are under my command. They work with energy, and they are here to support humanity. This information has never been released to the planet before, but we think you are now ready. Call these beings from the sky and ask them for the remembrance of why you are here.

You can also interact and play with clouds. For example, perhaps you want American culture to be understood in Japan. Talk to the clouds. They work in tandem with the wind. The wind can change cloud patterns to bring this understanding.

If you have a problem you cannot solve, talk to the clouds. The problem you have might have been resolved in other countries. The clouds will communicate with the clouds in other countries, and together with the wind, they will change

the cloud patterns. This understanding will be rained down energetically to the place where it is needed.

Why are we revealing this to you at this time? We strongly believe that it is time for humanity to connect the dots and use the support of the elements to bring better understanding and solutions to its problems using spiritual techniques. You can call on me to help. I will support you along with my helpers.

Your Supporting Energies Are Waiting to Be Discovered

Did you know that you can communicate with clouds and ask to be shown your individual pattern? For example, when you examine snowflakes, you can see that they are perfect and amazingly beautiful. Each snowflake is different. No two are exactly the same. Similarly, each human being has a sacred pattern. Ask the beings from the clouds to show you your specific pattern in the clouds. You might see it. You might feel it. You might even see it in your third eye. This can open up communication with the beings from the clouds and also with beings from outer space.

The Arcturians and Andromedans are benevolent beings who create on the ground the sacred patterns you call crop circles. If you visit a crop circle within seventy-two hours after it has been made, you can have a transcendental experience. You can communicate with these beings and ask that your own geometric pattern (or crop circle) be downloaded into you directly. If they can download a pattern onto the ground over such a long distance, they can do it for you too. You must call this forth and ask for it. These are your supporting energies waiting to be discovered.

Each human being has a sacred pattern. They are very highly developed and originated in the time of Atlantis. Ask for your own pattern to be downloaded into you by the Arcturians, Andromedans, and the beings in the clouds. Many people talk about the importance of Earth, but the sky and the clouds are equally important. They are the other side of the coin.

I can help and support you in manifesting this reality — to make a strong, healthy connection with the clouds. This can empower you, enrich your life, and most important, open you to higher perceptions and higher realities.

I am Aramm.

• • •

Creative Inspiration

Hello, my name is Agon. I am the Angel of Writing. Many of you want to express your views, your understanding, and your wisdom through writing. I can support you in that, for we can embed energies in your cells that can materialize as thoughts occurring to your brain to bring an idea forth.

Let us look at what thoughts really are. Many thoughts are about an event that happened in the past, and some are about what could happen in the future. But thoughts are not just about the past or the future or even about the present. They can be divine inspirations being downloaded into your mind.

Sometimes you see people committing hideous crimes. Others thought of them as good people. You might wonder what happened to them or whether this idea was from their own thought programming from the past (or the future) or a thought impregnated into them. It is often a thought impregnated into them. It was not a grudge they carried for a long time.

The point that we are trying to make is, when you call on us, we can impregnate completely new thoughts and ideas into your brain structure. These thoughts do not come from your past or from your future. They are completely new. They may include influences from the past, but most of the time, completely new ideas will be downloaded into you.

Many of you in the new consciousness feel you have missions. You have life purposes, for example, to bring forth an understanding in book form or in some other way. If you desire, we will work with you to manifest this reality. Although I work with writers, this creativity need not only be for writers. It could also include other means of creative expression. Are you ready to collect this energy?

You will see completely new thought patterns and ideas coming into you that you might never have thought of. Archangel Michael said that there are countless millions of angels, but unless you knock and ask, they cannot really support you. How were the writers of children's storybooks able to write their beautiful stories? From their imaginations? But who put the imagination into them?

The *Beauty and the Beast* and *Pocahontas* are incredible stories that are still loved by millions of children around the world. We inspired them. We work with your highest self. We will never interfere, but if asked, we will step into your reality.

• • •

Imagination versus Inspiration

Hello, this is Archangel Michael. Are there any questions?

What is the difference between imagination and this process?

This is a good question. Imagination is important. But imagination can only take you to a certain point. Imagination is very good, but it has limitations. You can imagine an experience you had in another lifetime or in another dimensional reality, but your imagination works from point to point. In our process, we place completely new, unadulterated energy into your energetic body, into your auric body. This will then take new roots. This is often completely new energy beyond your imagination. Or it may be in partnership with imaginative energy. Nonetheless, it will have a flavor of complete newness.

We have noticed that imagination can only take you so far. It has limitations. In our case, there are no limitations, for it is a new energetic imprint.

Would that be like the difference between a good story and something like* E.T.*, the movie by Steven Spielberg?

Yes. The movie *Close Encounters of the Third Kind* was given as a new energetic imprint. We know that Steven Spielberg has a brilliant mind and that he would be open to new ideas, so we impregnated this new thought form into him. He was able to draw it forth and, using his imagination, make it into a beautiful art form.

If you look at your old Hollywood movies, some good ones have been produced. Most of the movies are similar in character, except occasionally a movie comes out that completely touches everyone's heart. How did the writers come up with those brilliant new ideas? Between 80 and 90 percent of these films are the same, having shooting, killing, kidnapping, and so forth. There is very little difference in the storylines. But once in a while, a real story comes out that is completely outside the mainstream, and it makes a big impact, like the movie *Avatar*. It was completely new. It really touched people's hearts. How did the writer conceive of this? It is a completely new idea, not what Hollywood had been making, movies of guns and other things.

• • •

I have worked with a client who is a writer. She writes screenplays and theatrical plays. Her consciousness was very diffused, as if no one was home. I was trying to explain to her the difference between fantasy, daydreaming, and creating from her heart. I wonder whether you could touch on some of that.

This is Angel Agon. This is what we are talking about. If she were to write a play, it would be a play set in society. There would be nothing unusual about it, nothing that touches your heart and really stays there. Unless the new inspiration is implanted into her, she will continue producing the same kind of thing. It can be popular, but does it really touch somebody's heart? Perhaps not.

But she did not understand that her creative process involved daydreaming and fantasy as opposed to inspiration from the heart.

This is the problem with daydreaming. It works from point to point. That is it. You can only daydream to a certain point.

The effect of this on her was that it diffused her consciousness. It did not focus her.

It is very limited, exactly. But coming from the heart and calling on and working with angels will create completely new inspiration.

You could help inspire her if she were to ask?

Exactly — and all of you, bringing completely brand-new inspiration.

This is Angel Agon.

• • •

Preserve Wisdom and Intelligent Writing

Hello, my name is Ebed. All of you know me very well, for I work with all of you. I am a being who puts on many hats. This time I put on the hat of Ebed to speak with you. I am the angel who supports intelligent work, all forms of writing, and the preservation of wisdom in any form, whether it is art, music, sound, or oral transmission on a disk or even on a computer. There is much wisdom available, not just in the books you read or in lectures.

You can call on me to bring forth understanding from all sources where the wisdom to support humanity is taught, whether it is from a book, a person, a tree, or a cloud. Everything is alive and communicating, and everything comes from the Creator. Can we condense it into a form that supports humanity? I would say yes, definitely. You can call on me to bring you the exact wisdom that you need at this time in your life.

When new wisdom comes, it is very grand. People say they have waited for it. Perhaps you need some other wisdom to ground yourself so that you are able to access the new wisdom and utilize it. I provide the wisdom you need when you need it, tailored to your readiness to receive it and accept it.

Much information is available on the Internet — sometimes with wisdom

and sometimes not. It is not for you if it does not resonate. You can call forth the specific wisdom that you need. For example, Sister Jan and Brother Robert have been given an assignment by Archangel Metatron, who developed a program for healing adolescent children. But they were stumped, and said, "We do not know how to proceed. It looks interesting." Call on me. I will bring forth what you need.

For all my other brothers and sisters, ask, "What wisdom do I need to experience higher aspects of myself?" Asking is important because you often get stuck in one perspective and believe you have found your truth. Yes, you found it, but is this the wisdom and truth most applicable for today? You are a new person tomorrow and every moment of your life. You need higher vibrations of the truth, or maybe a completely new set of truths. I can provide it. Call on me. Ask for exactly what you want me to anchor into you: the truth that can support you to move to the next level, to experience another higher aspect of yourself.

Connect with the Wisdom within Mount Shasta

When you aspire to a goal, it is possible that your soul aspires to something completely different. Many things need to be done for your soul to bring forth this understanding. That is where I step in. I am directly connected to wisdom with the crystal located in the base of Mount Shasta. We have seen many teachers coming from Mount Shasta. We support them. Much wisdom comes from the universe, but Mount Shasta's energy gathers this wisdom, distills it, and transforms it into a practical application for the people of Earth.

If you are really observant, sometimes you will see messages coming directly from Mount Shasta. People of pure consciousness living in that area apply this universal wisdom in their everyday lives. Call on me, Ebed, to bring forth the wisdom that you need at this time.

When you were speaking, I saw a large tower reaching up into the sky and then some other geometrics. Was that something to do with Mount Shasta? Is that a way to access you? Is that how wisdom comes in?

Yes. You got it right, for I work with sacred geometries. What you saw is one aspect of the geometries. Good, you are opening your third eyesight.

I understand that Lemurians are residing underneath Mount Shasta. I would like to know whether there is a pyramid inside Mount Shasta.

There are three pyramids. There is a civilization. Adama and the ascension temples are at Mount Shasta. They have many visitors from outer space. Mount Shasta is important. I work independently, supporting the energy. What they bring out can support your evolution. But I work as an independent being.

I wish to share some of the secret with you. Who am I? [Pause.] I am Metatron.

Christine got it.

Christine got it; oh thank you.

I knew you right away.

Thank you. Thank you, Christine. Yes, I am Metatron. I bring understanding, exactly what you need at any time, if you call on me.

• • •

Activate Diplomacy for Effective Communication

Hello, my dear beloved family on the Earth plane. I am Angel Haaiaha. I am the angel of diplomacy and communication. If diplomacy is practiced properly, it can be very effective. Diplomacy is like the tire on a car. Because the tire is filled with air, a car rides smoothly. Diplomacy is the spice of communication. Without spices, you would eat bland food. When you add spices, it tastes better. In the same way, diplomacy complements human endeavors and communication.

Diplomacy can smooth differences, build bridges, create harmony, and most importantly, encourage effective communication. If there is good diplomacy, all problems can be solved.

Why do you think I am speaking to you today? Teachers and masters must be good diplomats. They are like ambassadors going to another country. The first job of ambassadors is to study the cultures of the people where they are going to understand the whole picture so that better communication and better friendship can take place. Since you are becoming diplomats of light, you will want to open the quality of diplomacy within you so that you will be better able to relate to the people who enter your energy field.

A diplomatic master will dispense energy and wisdom depending on the people coming into their energetic field. Good diplomats also keep their mouths shut when it is not appropriate to speak but important to listen. Good diplomats are very aware of situations every moment and take the perfect opportunity to speak the perfect words with the perfect energy to create change. Diplomacy is a skill you must cultivate, especially when you reach a certain level of mastery and are ready to step into the world to teach others.

Why is diplomacy important? Diplomacy builds bridges. It is collectively important for the planet, particularly from 2015 onward. Diplomacy will play a very big role in building unity consciousness, helping people who do not fully agree with each other to cooperate and create something new for the greater good of all. There will be intense diplomatic negotiations to prevent the further collapse of an economy or prevent a country from going to war.

Mediation for the Energy of Diplomacy

You might wonder where the energy of diplomacy is located in your body. This energy is in your tongue. Observe your tongue after swallowing something bitter. Similarly, diplomats will swallow difficulties in contentious situations for the greater good of everyone. This energy is under your tongue. It is a beautiful blue color.

Close your eyes, and focus your attention on the underside of your tongue. See three circles of blue light. They will start glowing. This glowing light will slowly enter your mind. Through your mouth, it will go into your ears and then into the meridian points going to your brain. It will slowly move to other parts of your body. Visualize this blue light resonating under your tongue, going up into your mouth, into your ears, into your brain, into your hands, and elsewhere.

This energy is now slowly stretching into your arms and into your fingers. See your fingers pulsing with this beautiful blue light. The tips of your fingers pulse with this blue light for this is the hand that will touch many, either through shaking hands or emitting energy.

Now see this light going into your third eye and shooting flames from your third eye, beautiful blue soothing flames. It goes into your auric field. People are drawn into your auric field through the power of attraction. When you are a diplomat, you will naturally attract people of that nature.

Breathe it in. Now slowly see energy coming from your third eye into your heart and moving clockwise. This light is spiraling into your heart and into your solar plexus because a diplomat must also be courageous. You can activate this energy anytime through your intention by bringing your attention to your tongue. Breathe it in three times, and see this energy being tied into your solar plexus. Breathe it in once again [pause] and once again [pause] and once again.

You may open your eyes at this time, dear family. Are you ready to be a diplomat?

Speaker 1: Yes, I can feel the quality of this. It is not unfamiliar to me. I have not always been a very good exhibitor of this quality of light, but it is there. I thank you for this. It is very beautiful.

Speaker 2: I could immediately feel the power of this beautiful channeling and the importance of being able to deliver a message with just the right recipe, the beautiful image of the spices of correct speech.

Speaker 3: It felt really good being activated, especially my fingertips. I feel that very strongly.

Speaker 4: This is such a powerful message. It is going to be a great tool for me to help others and myself.

You will have expanded energy in the coming months and years. You will meet many, many people. If you are good diplomats, you can put them at ease when they meet you, and they will be able to receive the message or the energy you transmit to them. You will build a bridge. How do you feel, Brother Mordechai?

Thank you for reactivating an area that I make attempts at. I have a lot of impatience that I have to get over.

Don't be hard on yourself. Your life's purpose is to remember what you already know inside. That is all.

There will be so many more people becoming unbalanced and so many people seeking answers. When you are a diplomat, you will be able to communicate with them at the right time, in the right way, and with the right words.

You can call on me anytime you need to communicate with me or fine-tune this energy. Perhaps you will be in a new city or in new surroundings to make a presentation. You will need to be in a place of courage and diplomacy so that you can do your work well. Call on me. Remember, this light is under your tongue.

Blessings. This is Angel Haaiaha.

CHAPTER SEVEN

Develop Environmental Connections

Archangel Sandalphon, Angel Shargum, Archangel Michael, Angels of the Seasons, Angel of Snow, Angel Amabael, Angel Sanaei, Angel of the Wind, Angel Ramuel, and Angel Horam Sho

This is Archangel Sandalphon. Good day, beloved family on the Earth plane. We are now watching Earth going through metamorphosis. You can play a larger role in molding and bringing balance into Mother Earth. She needs the support of every human being on the planet. She is overburdened by its population, and the conflicts are challenging and difficult for her. We ask you to do a simple exercise every day:

Activate your energy by breathing through your fingers and extending this to your palms. See yourself holding beautiful Mother Earth in both hands. If you want to make this more powerful, stand up with your legs apart, knees slightly bent. Imagine that you are holding Mother Earth in both your hands. This is very difficult to do. In ten minutes, your hands will become very heavy. In twenty minutes, it may be very difficult to even stand. You will feel the density and the heaviness of the energy of humanity. But if you are in a space of calmness and joy, you can emit these energies while you are holding Mother Earth. This pose can have a great impact on Earth at this time.

Show Appreciation for All Creation

We, the Angelic Kingdom, are surrounding Mother Earth. We are millions of angels, holding the energy coming from her. Wars and killings are very difficult for her. Many of her natural abilities for self-healing are depleted from bombings. Mother Earth was capable of taking care of herself, but with the great destruction (war and mining), her reserves and strength have become depleted. Uranium mining has depleted her brain capacity. Uranium is the material inside her brain. Imagine having a brain operation that removes some of your brain. You could not become whole again.

We ask all of you to support Mother Earth in your own way. When you drink a glass of water, bless Mother Earth who gave this gift to you. You could say, "By taking this water inside my body, I heal myself. I also heal Mother Earth, who is part of me."

Everything in creation needs acknowledgment and appreciation. You can test this idea yourselves. When you are not appreciated and when you are not greeted, how is your life? Without a greeting or appreciation coming from your friend, spouse, or children, you feel sad. Everything alive in creation should be appreciated. You like to be appreciated, and when that happens, you give back much more. Mother Earth needs you now.

Blessings, this is Archangel Sandalphon.

• • •

Water Is a Universal Connection

Hello, dear ones, I am the Angel of Water. Water is an interior part of humanity. When you compare the land mass and the water throughout the planet, you see there is much more water than land. Water plays a very important part in the creative process for this planet. When the planet was created millions of years ago, water was brought here. It did not just appear on the planet. The Creator requested that water be brought from another planet because the Creator was creating human beings with water. The intention was to create human beings with high water content so that they could do the work the Creator had intended.

Water holds your memories, your blueprints, and your life history. Imagine the water in a lake or a sea. Water holds vast records of wisdom and the history of the land. The water inside of your body holds your blueprint. What does water hold on the body of Earth? It holds similar things. When you know how to connect with water, especially water from lakes, rivers, and seas, then you can connect with the history of the planet.

There are many scientists, archaeologists, and anthropologists who look for evidence of lost civilizations and extinct animals, like dinosaurs, on Earth's surface, but rarely do they look into the history of water. Water was here before the animals or human beings were. Water has seen it all, and it holds these memories. Connect with that source, and you will discover your true history.

Water is very alive, especially flowing water. Water has many properties and is not the same in every location. What do I mean by "not the same"? It has the same fluidity and the same essence, but the vibrations are different. This is why you feel so refreshed when you drink water from certain places. You can determine which water sources have higher vibrations using the water inside your body. Make an energetic connection with that high-vibrational water to draw forth the memory, history, energy, vibrations, and light from that water into your physical body. Water can connect energetically with another source of water throughout this planet and beyond.

Here is a brief example: Lake Titicaca is on the border of Peru and Bolivia. It is one of the most sacred lakes. It is the place of one of the crystals from Atlantis called the thought crystal. Great spiritual beings live in the water there. It is also the place many souls visit before they are born to acclimatize to Earth's realities and atmosphere. A lot is going on in that part of the world. If you were to connect with Lake Titicaca, with the pure vibration that it holds, using the water within your body, then you would be able to connect with energy from that high source.

Some people who go to Lourdes and drink the water feel that they have been healed. Of course, faith plays a very big part in those healings. As for the water, it contains a high vibration due to the magnetics of the ground.

Mother Earth has provided certain places in her body where there is high vibration. You can connect with the vibration of the water. If you were to find out which water sources have higher vibrations, you could go there in your meditation and connect with these sources. You will not only remember more of yourself but also Earth's history, for the water has seen it all. The deep sea holds creations that came and vanished. The water has seen it all. It can bring forth understanding of what has been long lost and buried. We are not talking about 10,000 or 50,000 but millions of years ago.

Water can also regenerate. Using high-vibrational energy can have an effect on your physical body's organs. You can request that this high-vibrational water replace the water inside you, and there are body technicians who can support you in this. In many ways, it is like a resurrection of every place in your body.

How do we ask for the water within us to be replaced, and how often should we do that?

Only once. When you first make an energetic connection with the high-vibrational water around the world, you feel a connection, presence, or calling. You will immediately feel a difference within your being. You are creating a bridge of light, and you are connecting with the energetic source of a high vibration. You are plugging in. Distance does not matter because the wire is long enough. You can plug into a high vibration, a higher source of light.

Search the Internet, and you will find information about places where the water has a much higher-vibrational quality than other sources. You choose. For example, some places near the Grand Canyon are very pure. That is why certain areas are regulated. Large numbers of people cannot go because they want to keep the purity and high-vibrational energy.

Is the Sea of Galilee another place?

Many places have high-vibrational energy in the water. Look for them, and you will find them. Connect with them, and you will see a huge difference in your life. They will help you remember, and connecting with water can also help you understand Earth's history, because the water has seen it all — more than anything else.

Connect with High-Vibrational Water

I read that we receive information from Divine Source through water circuits in our bodies. Is that correct?

They support you, very much so. Water is very much alive. It is easy for beings of light to communicate with you through water rather than through your mind because when they communicate through water, you are more receptive. Your body is full of water. Divine inspiration can be installed in water, and then you receive it intuitively.

Let us say you want to make a change in your life. Project the intention of what you want to change into water you are about to drink, and ask the water to circulate throughout your being and flush out your resistance to change. You have a better chance of releasing it this way than by just using your mind. Many people try to use their minds to release bad habits, bad patterns, or bad behaviors. They do affirmations or visualizations. All these support a little bit, but the best way is to use visualizations along with flushing their bodies with water they have charged with their intentions. Water rules your body.

We have sacred baths and sacred ceremonies of healing, and we go to the waters to be healed. It seems to me this is exactly what you are talking about. You immerse yourself in sacred water that has been blessed.

Exactly. One of the rituals John of God[1] encourages is to go to a waterfall and ask the water to take the issue you are carrying.

There are angels at waterfalls. Is that correct?

Exactly.

I have seen some angels. They were not like humans. They were more like sparkles.

Exactly. They are more like light.

It seems that as we know our bodies, the water on Earth can empower us to know the universe, and we become one with Earth as we do that.

Of course. The purpose of this book is to bring understanding of how angels can be called forth to support humanity. The support we are trying to bring forth is working with angels who can help you remember and know the God that you seek in your physical body first by understanding the physical body. You are right. Bring people back to their bodies so that they can know more and remember more.

Is our water connected with all the water in the universe? Could one access a star system that has water?

The water in other star systems is similar, but it has a different texture. It can

1. João Teixeira de Faria (born June 24, 1942), known also as João de Deus (John of God), is a medium and psychic surgeon. He is based in Abadiânia, a small town in the state of Goiás, southwest of Brasília, where he runs the Casa de Dom Inácio de Loyola (the Casa), a spiritual healing center where he sees thousands of visitors every week from all over the world.

be thicker or more fluid or have different energy. But yes, you can connect with the water systems of other planets.

Which planet would you suggest we connect with for a high vibration and rejuvenation?

You could connect with the lake in Arcturus, the water system of Shamballa, or the water source in Tellos. Or you could even request the White Brotherhood's lake that the ascended masters use. You could call Saint Germain for a water source, for he is a master alchemist of water. Work with these beings: Call forth, connect, and transform. You must seek the new truth. Work with it; you are capable of accessing this information.

Would it be appropriate to ask you to bless our drinking water, or should we ask for something more specific?

First, you must appreciate the water you are going to drink with the energy of your own I Am presence. Then you can call on me to ask that the water you are going to drink be connected with the water source at the universal level of Lord Melchizedek. Visualize this energy going into your water for maybe a minute or two, for there is a water source on the universal level. When you drink this water, it heals your entire physical body holographically; one part of a hologram heals the whole.

All the masters could be completely in touch with their physical bodies and be completely aware of the water within them. Some people talk about being aware of their bodies, but how many people have been able to maintain these high vibrations or even know about them — a few perhaps — to truly experience awareness through their bodies? This is done with water. Ask the water.

My understanding is that the water is connected to our emotional bodies. Can you clarify that?

This is true, of course. If the water inside of you is connected with high-vibrational water from another place, what happens to your emotions? You would be in a much better place emotionally. You would be clearer, more vibrant, and more at peace. Energy would move through your emotional body in a much more refined way. Yes, you are connected to your emotional body through water.

Call on me, the Water Angel. I will give my name to you. You can call me Shargum. I am not female nor male. Since water holds emotions, people think of me as feminine, but I am neither. I am the whole.

Is there a way of activating consciousness in water for regular baths or showers?

Yes, of course. First, sending your energy into the water creates a molecular structure that will change the water. You can also make a fist, extend your pinky finger, and draw clockwise circles just above the surface of the water. That can also change the water molecules. And you can work with the Water Angels to energize the water. Their vibration can help you very much.

Ask them to clear the impurities in the water. Processing facilities, chemicals, and the thoughts of the people who process the water cause these impurities. Water carries a lot of energy, so you need to influence it and purify it.

Become aware of your water. Consciously communicate with it, and then bathe in it. It will heal you. Most humans are not aware of this. They just turn the knob for the faucet, and the water is there. But water goes through so much processing from different sources before it comes to your faucet. It is processed with many materials, using metals, plus the thoughts of the people who work with the water.

This is called living consciously — being aware and conscious of everything. Then you also become aware that you have the capacity to bring change, to bring the water you use to your level of vibration.

I am a massage therapist, and I do water treatments. Should I do this for my clients? Should I explain what I am doing to them?

It could help them of course. You could ask them whether they would like to try it out. But most people are very stubborn. They do not want to change. You could tell them that this process can help them because you have worked with it, and then they may choose it.

Some people might see it as hocus-pocus.

Of course, all truths are considered hocus-pocus until it becomes real to people through their own experiences.

This is Angel Shargum.

• • •

Thank you. This is Archangel Michael. We are bringing understanding to support your life. Like anything else that is new, some will reject it and some will accept it. Work with it to see whether it supports you in your own life. Working with angels can truly have a transformational effect.

Our intention for this book is to bring awareness of angels to your conscious level so that you will call them forth and work with them. This will transform your lives and Earth simultaneously. Angels are here to be called forth, and when you call them forth, transformation can occur much more quickly than working by yourself.

You have heard of miracles being performed by angels. Why wait for a disaster to call for angels? Why not call them on a daily basis and become friends with them? You will see the difference when you do this.

• • •

Align with Seasonal Frequencies for Balance

Hello. We are the Angels of Seasons. The seasons were created for a very specific purpose: to create rhythm within human beings. They are an example to humanity about life, death, decay, and resurrection. When you observe the change of seasons, you see an ending of one thing and the beginning of something else.

Everything in the universe is cyclical in nature, but there are specific vibrations and energies in each season. Some of you know about this. You see spring as a new beginning. Winter is a time to rest. Fall is a time of harvest. Summer is a time of ripening, leading to harvest. Each season has its own colors, its own vibration, and more importantly, its own rhythm of sound.

When you work in harmony with these sounds, you will easily be able to incorporate the seasonal changes within yourself. Many people feel different emotions in their bodies during the change of seasons, resulting in mood swings. Some people can even become depressed or suicidal. In Japan, some people begin to withdraw and become sad and depressed at the change of seasons. Suicides can increase as a result, which is seen in other countries too.

Music is emitted at the change of seasons, a frequency, or harmony. Tune into this frequency. Ask to integrate with this frequency. You do not need to know what the frequency is. When you call this forth during meditation, you will see angels who support this change of season. Integrate this energy into your consciousness, and see a thread of light going through your solar plexus, deep into the energy of the season.

For example, visualize fall energy as beings of light holding fall colors in their hands. Extend a light energy from your solar plexus into the colors of fall and back into yourself through your solar plexus, spreading through you so that you are imbued with the colors of fall within your being. This energizes all your bodily organs with fall and reharmonizes you with the rhythms of nature that are already in you.

You can do this for each season to help you be in complete harmony. You will be able to take advantage of seasonal changes without going through emotional ups and downs.

It is the same with the other cycles of nature — the cycles of the Moon, the equinoxes. Some people are afraid of eclipses, but you can utilize these energies for powerful transformation. You can become very strong in these energies, for they are very powerful. You need to attune to them.

The bodily rhythm of a child is more in harmony with the changing seasons than an adult. They do not go through as many behavioral changes during these times as adults do. When you are in tune with the changing seasons, your thinking will be different. The way you act and respond will be different. The way you eat will also be different. Connect with the essence of the devas for each season. At each change of season, you can ask, "What can I do during this changing season within my being to better balance myself?" Your soul needs this and waits for you to make this request.

When you align yourself with the changing seasons, you flow with the universal rhythm. You flow with the rhythm of your body. You can utilize this energy to be in a better space. When you are in a better space, you have better energy. There will be much more flow in your life.

People are affected by seasonal changes. Winter affects people greatly, much more than they realize. They bundle up. They wear many layers of clothing. The best way to align with a season is to align with its energy. Then you will be able to go through the season easily.

We are the Angels of Seasons.

• • •

Cold Supports Awakening

Hello, family. I am the Angel of Snow. There is a reason why some places get more snow than others. People choose to be born in cold places for a reason — cold supports awakening. Perhaps a soul has been trying to awaken its personalities for many lifetimes but never awakens. It chooses to be born in a cold place so that the energy, the atmosphere, and the climate will support awakening. Does awakening happen in hot places, such as Africa or the Middle East? No, only countries that have both cold and hot places.

Some souls have chosen to be born in cold places to break certain behavioral patterns. You can communicate with me, the Angel of Snow, and ask that the lessons you have come here to learn be brought into your awareness and that

you not be too affected by the cold. If you really look at what cold is, it is what you think about it. For a child of eight to ten, playing in the snow is fun. An older person will not usually go out.

You can work with the essence of snow because the essence of fire comes from the essence of snow. That means snow contains fire. You can call forth the power of fire, the heat power from snow. Many of your recent saints are now doing so in India, the Tibetan Himalayas, and other sacred places.

In your meditation, call on me and ask for the essence of heat to be anchored into you, and you will feel warmth coming into your solar plexus. This is embedded deep inside the snow. Then ask for this energy in your solar plexus to be distributed throughout your body, and you will feel warm. We encourage you to try this. This is how the ancient shamans lived.

• • •

Connect with the Four Seasons

Hello, my name is Amabael. I am an angel of the winter season. Some people refer to winter as Old Man Winter. Some might refer to it as Young Maiden Winter. I work with the elements of winter.

Did you know that every human body carries all four seasons within? Winter is in your physical body; so are summer, spring, and fall. Do you think only chakras affect you? The four seasons live within you, and you can acclimatize yourself to connect with them. Then you will be in tune with the seasonal changes because you will become the season yourself.

The four seasonal cycles are connected to the number 4. Four is a very big number. In some cultures, 4 is called the number of death. The number 4 is connected to the four elements, four seasons, and four cycles of life — birth, growing up, old age, and death.

Close your eyes and imagine a square around you. In the middle of the square, there is a circle with the dial of a clock. The four corners of the square represent the four seasons. See the hands of the clock passing through all four seasons. Ask for the dial to be set to your time frame, even when it is a different season.

How did the ancient ones live during extreme weather conditions? Master Jesus taught how to tune into the seasons in the body. During a hot summer day, you can relax and cool your body. Some Christian and Islamic monks wear black robes even during the hottest summer days. They know how to adjust their bodies to the four seasons. Certain yogis and masters can set their dials to breathe in and bring warmth into their bodies.

Where would you like to set your dial at this moment? If you are in a cold place, you could need more warmth.

Make your intention to set your dial on summer, and breathe in the energy of summer. Breathe the summer's warmth into your body, and feel the energy going into the palms of your hands, first into your skeleton, then into your legs, your brain, and your head.

Open your eyes now. How do you feel now? Do you feel some energy at all?

Speaker 1: I feel peacefulness. I feel in harmony with myself and with the environment.

Speaker 2: I feel harmony and a humming energy.

Speaker 3: I feel a warming.

You can feel the difference no matter what season you are in because the seasonal forces exist in your body. You can tap into the energy of any season. I will help you with this. You can regulate your body rhythm yourself and be in harmony with your body.

This is Angel Amabael.

• • •

Call on the Love of Flowers

My name is Sanaei. I am the flower angel. You can call on me before you go to sleep to bring you the love and comfort that you did not receive that day. If you had a rough day and you want some tender loving care, call on us, especially if you are alone or do not get love from your family or others. Ask us to administer the beauty, grace, and love that flowers emit.

The plant and flower kingdoms emit frequencies and vibrations that are very pure and innocent, like that of a baby. Ask us to infuse this energy into you, and through this, you can awaken to the inner part of you that can give you the same feeling.

• • •

Breathe Fully

I am the Angel of the Wind. Everybody knows about the wind, but hardly anyone acknowledges the wind. Without the wind, no one could be alive — no humans, no plants, no animals. We feel we need more recognition and acknowledgment. That is why we speak now.

Who uses the wind properly, and what does "properly" mean? First of all, no one breathes fully. They do not take full breaths to fill their lungs. Most people take very shallow breaths.

Just imagine that you are breathing. Can you imagine the wind inside you?

Have you heard the song "The Wind Beneath My Wings"? What can it do for you? It can make you fly and feel a sense of freedom. Call on us and work with us, the wind element, and many will be healed.

Blessings, I am the Angel of the Wind.

• • •

Support Earth's Small Creatures

Hello, my name is Ramuel. I am one of the angels who supports the small creatures who crawl and run on Mother Earth's body. There are infinite numbers of beings in the ground. All birth the love of Creator. Human beings do not see them or really understand them. They are part of creation, and we support them to survive so that they can do the work they have come here to do.

These creatures are in service to Mother Earth, and they are essential for the whole to be completed in its perfection. But as the human population increases and takes more land, many of these little ones are disappearing. Chemicals used in agriculture are killing a large number of these beings.

There are also many beings in the deepest part of the oceans, and they keep the oceans clean. Our task is to support these beings with much love and energy so that they can multiply and grow. More deforestation is happening. Call on

me if you want to understand why these beings are here on this planet, for they can share their wisdom and their truth with you.

For example, ants are always busy doing something. They are a very well-organized society, and your scientists know this. You can call on their essence to organize a structure in your own life. They have many beautiful stories to tell. If you call on me, I will enlighten your mind about the purpose of these little beings.

These creatures will help you find treasures and gems in the little things of your life. Most people find pleasure only in the bigger things of life and discard the little things. Little things are a treasure trove. They are littered with treasures, but your eyes are focused on other things.

I can help you open a new perspective to find the little treasures in your life. And the little treasures make up the big treasure. There is beauty, there is grace, and there is perfection in the little things in your life — and in the little ones on the ground.

Blessings.

• • •

Send Your Energy via Flight

Hello, dear family. We are the angels who support all flying beings, from birds to bees, everything that flies. All flying beings are important in the overall energy

configuration of Earth, for they carry specific vibrations from place to place, and they work completely in harmony with the element of the wind.

You have seen birds flying in formation or going in one direction every morning and then returning in the evening. You could say they are going to find food, but maybe they have other reasons. They are distributors of energy, especially when they are flying in formation.

Why do you think water mammals migrate at certain times? Scientists say this is because of warm currents and cold currents. That is only one reason. Water mammals have accumulated certain energy, and they distribute it through their migration routes and deposit it where they stay for certain lengths of time.

Everything in the universe has a purpose, but humans rarely ask why. What is the purpose of these things? You can communicate with flying birds and deposit your energy into them, and they will carry that energy (especially love or wisdom) and drop it where it is needed. On the return trip, they bring the wisdom or the energy you need. Some of the greatest teachers, like Master Jesus, watched the birds. If you look in your history, you will see who helped Howard Carter find the Tomb of King Tutankhamun.[2] He searched for many years, but he could not find it. He had a bird with him, and this bird told him where to

2. See T. G. H. James, *Howard Carter: The Path to Tutankhamun* (New York: Saint Martin's Press), pp. 250-51, about Howard Carter's canary.

look. Birds have this capacity. Get in touch with them.

Who do you think planted the idea that people can fly? Birds had been relaying this information for a long time until the two Wright brothers got an idea that finally led to sustained controlled flight.

You can call on birds to support you. Find their migration patterns and ask them to bring you the awareness that you need or the practical application of wisdom to solve some of life's problems.

Our angelic name is Horam Sho. Blessings.

• • •

Ask the Universe

This is Archangel Michael. The birds taught Saint Francis how to communicate with other animals. He is the patron saint of animals. It is time to awaken and see all the things given by the Creator to support humanity. Look at everything in the universe and ask, "What is the purpose of a rabbit? Why was the rabbit — or an earthworm or a tick — brought here?"

Even the mosquitoes?

Yes, or the cockroach. When you start looking at everything as a part of creation with a specific purpose, you will see the beauty in everything, including mosquitoes. They play their parts.

It has truly been a joy to communicate with all of you. I hope that you all enjoy this interesting wisdom brought forth by all these enlightened beings who are in awe of humanity and work to support you.

We are bringing forth angels people are not aware of, for it is our understanding that once human beings come to understand the role of angels in all walks of their lives and are able to work with them, a truly incredible transformation can happen very quickly. It is time for humanity to completely understand their true purpose for being here on the planet.

CHAPTER EIGHT

Revitalize Your Health and Well-Being

Archangel Metatron, Angel Ra-v-s, Archangel Michael, Angel Shamiel, Angel Shanome, Angel Och, Angel Wanfa-so, and Angel Mansu

This is Archangel Metatron. Angels have truly been part of the human experience from time immemorial. When you call on us and work with us consistently, you will see a change in your personal circumstances. We are the emissaries of the Creator in full form. A time will come when we will visually appear to human beings.

If you study the Bible, you will see we appeared before Mother Mary when she was with child. We walked with her when she was ready to give birth. How is it possible that some people can see us and some cannot? The energy of angels has always existed, but some are able to focus on it, see us, and work with us. Whatever you focus on, you draw forth into your life, including God and angels.

You have read stories of angels protecting you during important times, shielding you, bringing forth understanding and love when they are most needed, and comforting people in times of stress and difficulties. Spend a few minutes a day communicating, meditating, and calling angels forth. Let this be your new prayer from now on, and you will see how your life will shift in a very short time.

You can even call on the angels of the body to administer to the needs of your body energetically. Did you know that you could call forth the immune system angels inside your body? You can call forth your bone angels too. There is so much to be understood about angels. You can call on the blood angels to purify your blood and make it consistent for optimum health — so your blood pressure is not too high and not too low, maintaining its purity.

There are also angels who work with the brain. Slowly, human beings will see that angels are there in every part of their lives — in every situation, every experience, and for all of creation. Now to you, my friend, there is also an angel for beards.

Do we have his name?

His name is Sahm. Call on him. The beard has a great consciousness. Why do you think many masters grew beards? The lady masters have long hair. The beard carries the wisdom you have inside you.

Blessings. This is Metatron.

• • •

Energize Your Food with Its Original Consciousness

Hello, my friends, I am Angel Ra-v-s, the Angel of Digestion. Your digestive organs are doing a magnificent job. Imagine all the different foods you eat every day. It takes a tremendous effort to manage these foods and digest them. You can overtax your digestive system by consuming food that is not the best for your body, but that is not our judgment to make. Have you ever thanked your digestive system for doing such a marvelous job? Every organ is important. Imagine if you did not have a digestive system.

We produce the chemicals inside your digestive system so that what your body consumes is processed and recycled. This supports you by sending energy and nutrition to different parts of your body. We are called digestive technicians.

We also work closely with other beings in your physical body, particularly beings who work with your emotions.

The human body has been called a group energy. Your body is composed of many beings. There are beings in your body who work with your hands. There are beings working with your emotional body. Emotions are mostly stored in your belly.

There are many beings, or energies, in your body. If all these beings are happy, you are in a happy state of mind. There are beings who regulate such things. We can communicate with these beings, but our work is principally with food digestion, because the food you eat contains consciousness.

Everything you eat is of God-consciousness — the vegetables, meat, and wine. Everything is consciousness. When you consume food, you eat it to extract this consciousness. We take this consciousness and send it to your pineal gland. This is why you are what you eat, for food plays a very big part in the composition of your consciousness.

Before you eat, energize your food to bring it into its original consciousness and communicate with us, requesting that your food contains its original consciousness. For example, many ingredients in your salad go through many processes before they become salad. We can bring all the ingredients of your salad into their original consciousnesses before they became a salad. Then you will have a higher concentration of this God consciousness. Of course, our duty — our work — is to support you in healing. We will send this higher consciousness into your pineal gland.

In earlier times, many spiritual beings lived on prana because the food they had to eat did not have consciousness. They were not aware of this. They only wanted to have higher-consciousness food. But now you do not have to refrain from eating. You can eat the same food you eat now, but talk to us before you start eating to bring the consciousness into these foods. Then there will be no difference between you and people who live on prana. You will be taking the vital energy from these foods, and you will start to see your intake of food diminish. You will carry the pure prana from the ingredients before it became food.

Good day to you. I am the Angel of Digestion.

• • •

This is Archangel Michael. By performing the method described, you will start seeing your food intake become less because the original consciousness of the plant is already in the food. It is the original consciousness, which is pure vibration. You take in very little and your stomach becomes full.

I bless my food with my hands before eating. You're saying we should ask that each ingredient be restored to its original consciousness?

Exactly. In three days, you will see a difference. As you know, the foods you eat have very little consciousness because of how they are manipulated. Pure food is still available in places where very few chemicals are used. This still contains good consciousness. Again, dear brother Mordechai, your rabbis and your people know about this.

This is kosher food.

Celebrate as You Cook

I do a lot of cooking. People could say I am a chef because what I cook is delicious, but when I cook, I put happiness into the food. I sing ...

The thoughts you carry are very important when you cook. So celebrate while you cook. Sing and dance and cook. This is very good for you. Singing is wonderful, because when plants are cut without their permission, they feel sad and depressed. Imagine that you are sad and someone comes along and sings to you. Would you not feel better? You would feel love and support.

Before you heat your food, ask that it be restored to its original consciousness, and you will experience the difference. What you think as you cook is absolutely critical, because if you think cooking is a chore, then there is no energy in the food at all. So blessings should be done before cooking starts, before you sit down at the table.

While making a salad, I was told to use a very sharp knife, as sharp as a scalpel, because you don't feel it when you cut your own skin with a sharp razor. Is it true that vegetables feel less pain when you use a much sharper blade?

Use any knife, because the vegetable has already been cut before. The best way of cutting is not direct cutting but cutting in a slanted position. When you go to the doctor and they put a needle straight into your hand, you feel more pain. When they slant the needle, you have less pain. It is the same thing. Vegetables are part of God's creation and are very alive.

Are the beings and angels who are in charge of digestion and emotions actually inside our bodies?

They are inside and outside; most of the angels are part of an energy group. This is why you are called a group energy. They are part of this energy setup. They work through your etheric body.

You work with your chakras, but how about working with your etheric chakras? These are not just the physical chakras. You will have an incredible amount of healing and light coming into you. Call on your etheric chakras to fully activate your chakras in the physical.

• • •

Use Sound to Manifest, Heal, and Comfort

This is Angel Shamiel, the Angel of Heavenly Sound and Heavenly Music. In many paintings, you see angels blowing trumpets. Yes, there is angelic harmony and angelic music. With every birth, there is an angelic choir. Some people who have had deep spiritual experiences hear the choir when attending the birth of a child. The same thing happens during death. There is singing and angelic sounds. Music is as much a part of our side as it is your side. Many ascended masters are particularly fond of angelic music.

There is music for every expression and experience of life. In many cultures, people sing. There is music for joyful celebrations as well as death and for many occasions in between. There is also music on our side for every expression. And your body has music. Your cells emit a sound, or frequency. When you combine the music of the angelic realm, called heavenly sound, with the frequencies of the sound you are emitting, a chemical process of healing and transformation is created. This is why sound healing can be effective. The sounds from other realms are of a higher-vibrational energy, and they override the energy or sound you bring out through your body.

Every thought you have is energetic and has a sound frequency attached to it. This energy can become embedded in your body. When you are aware of your thoughts and emotions, they manifest; immediately call forth the angelic choir, and ask them to bring their sounds to your cellular structure.

You can call me and my support team to bring my angelic sound into your home and anchor it there, and through the power of intent, activate this sound. Many great masters have invited Master Saint Germain to anchor his violet flame into their homes permanently. This anchoring is only granted once your heart is very pure. Saint Germain has graciously supported people in this way, for their homes become permanently purified by the violet flame. In the same way, you can invite angelic sound to be permanently anchored in your home. Everything in your home is energized.

You can call me and my support team to bring forth songs that are unique to you. The song could be a letter, a word, or a tone. We work as a unified force field with your support team and in complete harmony with your I Am presence.

We are very aware of what is happening in your life and what you need at any given moment.

There are sounds to be used for manifesting your reality. There are sounds to release souls from their physical bodies when the time is right. Sometimes a soul is ready to transition, but human beings still hold on because of their earthly attachments. There are sounds that can be used for a gentle soul release, and the attachment to the body will be removed.

There are sounds that can be used before surgery so the patient is in a state of heightened awareness of the healing energies being given by their guides. When people go to the hospital, their guides are at work. They know medicine can deplete the energy level. There are sounds to maintain the same frequency before they go to the hospital for surgery. Master Jesus often used sound in his healing.

You can request sounds for different purposes. I will give you a sound that can be used to manifest a desired intent that comes from the purest part of you.

Please close your eyes, and make a gentle fist. Let your thumb be on top of your fingers. Bring your fist in front of your heart, and breathe. When you make this sound, focus on the sound and your heart, not on your fist. The sound is "thargumasa." As you do this, you will feel vibrations from your heart going into your fist, "thargumasa." Practice this sound to support you to manifest a desired reality. This is a supportive sound recognized by your soul.

There are sounds for great voyages. In ancient times, voyages were fraught with many difficulties and challenges. Many voyagers knew they might never return to see their families. How were they guided? Some would say they used the stars. This is true, but they were also in harmony with the water spirits, Mother Earth, and spirits of navigation and voyage. There is one sound that you can use for smaller voyages, to keep you safe, and to be in harmony, in the flow. The sound is *Aramsa. Aramsa. Aramsa. Aramsa.*

There are also sounds that can help release attachment to the physical body so that the soul can depart on its intended journey. That sound is something like this: *Hamyaha.* The simple meaning is, "I am complete now. I can depart now since I am complete. I am complete." If you do this sounding for someone who is ready to die and your intention is to wish him or her dead, it will not work. This sounding is only effective in the proper perspective; these are spiritual tools used only for the highest good. When patients are deliberately kept alive using technical methods in a hospital, it does not serve any purpose for their souls. It only serves the egos of the doctors and the community. You have heard about situations in which people are kept alive in vegetative states for thirty or forty years, and it is done "in compassion." This has nothing to do with compassion, only with human ego and misunderstanding.

We go into each room in the hospital and make the sound *hamyaha* three to four times. The vibration of this sound anchors that energy. Sound travels around the room and clears away all energies. These sounds are powerful. The room is cleared, and the things in the room (the furniture, the curtains, and so on) are all aligned at the quantum level and are energized, are supported, and feel loved. Everything needs to be appreciated. Comfort a person with sound.

Here is your angelic calling card. Make this a part of your own mantra. Master Djwhal Khul taught, "I am the soul. I am the monad." You can say, "I am this sound. I am this soul. I am this sound. I am this soul." When you work with sound, all your bodily systems are affected, all the tissues, organs, and bones — the entire skeletal structure — and your other bodies in other dimensions.

You see suffering in people in all parts of the world. You can use sound to bring forth encouragement and support for these people. You do not have to go there physically. Just use sound, and they will receive it and feel it. Although you may emit it simply with a whisper, sound can travel for quite a distance. The energetic vibration of sound can travel to other continents and sometimes even to outer space. How does this work? It works through golden light waves. These will transport whatever sound you make and deposit it where you intend to send it.

There are golden lightbeings created by the Creator in complete support of humanity. You can call these golden lightbeings to support you, to have more golden energy in you. It is as if they are spinning a wheel of golden light. They are not only working for the reality of Earth but other realities as well. They mostly work for the people of Earth. You can ask for your specific frequency of golden light from golden lightbeings. In your meditation, call on me and my support team to bring forth your unique sound and also sounds for healing humanity: *Saaa. Saaa. Saaa.*

I would like to give you a sound that can be used to bring comfort to people in war zones, like refugees in the Middle East. The sound is simple: *Sakth.*

Close your eyes, and place your hand on your solar plexus. Make this sound with your hand on the solar plexus, focusing your attention on your third eye and the back of your neck: Sakth. Sakth. Sakth. Sakth. Sakth.

This is a universal sound. When you call this sound, many beings and supporting energies flock to its vibration. They will do their part to help heal people. This energy is a calling signature for these beings who are there to support people during this kind of crisis. There is support energy for every situation, such as when someone dies instantly. Even during a great time of tragedy, there are energies that can be called for support. This is a calling signature: *Sakth. Sakth.* It means, "I call on the gods who can help the suffering masses to help us at this time." Legions of angels and others will flock to the place where the energy of healing is needed.

Please remember this, dear ones: Along with your individual path, you must also constantly support your brothers and sisters. This is requisite for your ascension. It is not one or the other. Both are integral parts of your ascension process.

***Sakth* and *aramsa,* are these from an ancient language?**

They are not from an Earth language, but we are trying to bring this understanding to you through Earth language.

Access Your Unique Sound

How can I access my individual sound?

Bring your attention to your solar plexus. Put your hand there, just breathe, and say, "I bring forth the sound within my being." And let any sound come out. Anything. Open your mouth, and let any sound come out.

What I seem to receive from inside myself is the sound *Om*.

What this says to you is that sound can help and support you, but this is not your original sound. This is a sound that can support you very much at this time in your life, and it can also bring a lot of spiritual energy into you. You are very much connected to this energy, for you know this energy.

May I give you another sound? Close your eyes, breathe through your third eye, and sound: *Sah. Sah. Sah. Sah. Sah.* Can you feel the vibration in your third eye?

I feel as though my third eye is blocked at the moment. Sorry.

Rae's third eye is now throbbing. *Sah.* When you call forth this sound, focus your attention on your solar plexus. If any sound comes out, it will be the sound of what is necessary for you at this time. This sound can shift and change as you shift and change. But we encourage you to practice this for the next thirteen days, and we guarantee this simple exercise will allow a sound to come through that is unique to you. The new sound will immediately uplift your vibration. You will feel it inside and out, and you will not be able to deny it.

When I am in my garden, I always look for a sound to help Mother Earth heal and to bring sound to the beings who are helping the plants grow. What is the best way for me to find that sound?

Close your eyes, dear one, and bring your attention to the top of your head and make this sound now: *Gunn. Gunn. Gunn. Gunn. Gunn.* How do you feel?

It's almost as if the vibration within me is changing.

Exactly. When you do this sound, you are becoming more balanced and more in harmony with yourself. Then you are in the natural flow with everything in the universe, including the beings and energies in the ground. That is the best thing you can do to bring healing to Earth. Start with *gunn.* You will shift, and you will feel a sense of peace, balance, clarity, harmony, and of course, love. This energy will naturally go out through you. You will transfer it into the ground. It will be like a healing balm for Mother Earth, and all the beings who support the plants will feel this vibration coming from you. *Gunn.*

I have had two experiences on two different beaches in which I heard a choir from the rocks. The rocks were singing the glory of God. One was on the island of Iona and the other was on Lake Huron. Did I hear these because of the holiness of the land in those places?

Everything in the universe, especially in nature, constantly sings the glory of God. You were able to open up and listen in those places. Everything in nature sings all the time, including the trees in your own garden.

Here is an example: If you want to find a book, you go to the library. You know you can find a book in the library, but when you enter the library, you find a beautiful room. There are many paintings. Your eyes first go to the paintings, a statue, or maybe a stuffed animal, whatever. After you have examined everything, you go to the bookshelf and find the book. Did the book just appear there? No, the book was always there from the time it was created. By focusing your attention, you found the book.

The universe is always singing in harmony. When you are ready, you will be able to hear it. In certain power centers, the harmony is amplified, and you are more open in such places. Everything in the universe is always singing the glory of creation, except for human beings. Does this answer your question, dear one?

Yes, very clearly. Thank you.

I withdraw at this time. This is Angel Shamiel.

• • •

Essential Oils Increase Vitality and Healing

Hello, my name is Shanome. I am the Angel of Divine Smell. We have never spoken to human beings before, but the window of opportunity is now here, and I have been invited by Archangel Michael to speak with you.

What does "divine smell" mean, and how can it be applied in your life? This is simple. Smell, by its very nature, has the capacity to help you remember. Say that you are walking down a street in Jerusalem, Japan, or the United States of America, and you pass an old-fashioned bakery. The oven is on; breads and cookies are being baked. You sense the smell. Do you feel good about it, dear ones?

Yes.

Why is this so? This is because it helps you remember your home and the love of your mother and family. In a nanosecond, you are taken back to a place of love, and you feel good. Smell has this capacity. In a nanosecond, it can travel to all parts of your body.

Your skin is breathing. The hair on your skin is breathing. They take in nutrients not only from food but also from what is breathed in. You can treat yourself with smells through your skin. You can apply them directly to your skin, or you can place a few drops in a bowl of water, and say, "I am going to breathe in this smell through my skin and through the hairs of my skin." Immediately, the hairs and the skin will become more open and awake, and when they are awake, the muscles and tissues underneath the skin will also start awakening.

Smell can dissolve energies that have become stuck inside your physical body. These energies become condensed, like matter. In the future, smells will be used to teat tumors and other masses growing inside the physical body treated with smell. Sound will be used, and so will smell. Both will play an equal part.

When you wake up tomorrow morning — before you eat your breakfast or even have a cup of tea — put one or two drops of any essential oil on a tissue or a small plate, and breathe it in a few times. You will feel a sense of vitality the whole day, and your need to drink coffee or tea will be diminished. You will be full with the smell. You will still enjoy coffee because your tongue and body have built up a taste. It will take some time, but you will disconnect from the craving. You will drink coffee because you enjoy it, not because you crave it.

Most of the time you eat food because you do not remember who you really are. Many masters remember who they are, and they do not eat food. They eat occasionally because it is a joy to eat, but they do not eat often. You will feel a

sense of well-being when you do this simple activity every morning before you drink coffee. When you drink coffee or tea, it affects the dynamics in your cells. They go into overdrive.

Experiment to Identify a Smell That Supports You

You can ask for the heightening of your senses so that you can feel the beautiful fragrance of divine smell within you. You have a gland of smell inside your body. It is located between your temple and your left ear, just underneath the hairline. Ask that this gland be stimulated and activated once again. Imagine a smell to induce birth, a smell for an easy death without fear, or a smell to calm fighting between two people.

Some department stores in America and Japan release a smell before the store is opened. This is an artificial smell created by an American scientist, and it makes the customers stay in the store longer so that they will spend more money.[1] If smells can influence you to make more purchases, can you imagine how smells could work in conflict management? They activate the gland within you, and you fall in love with yourself.

1. Learn more about how scents influence behavior at http://healthland.time.com/2013/12/16/my-nose-made-me-buy-it.

There are tales from Indian mythology in which a king meets a fisherman's daughter.[2] He falls in love with her instantly. She does not smell like the fisherman. She smells like a beautiful, soft, fragrant rose.

Which essence would you recommend to fully energize us first thing in the morning?

Play with two or three essences. Use whatever essence you have in your house. Use one tomorrow to see its effect, and use another the next day. Use what you have, work with them, and you will see the differences.

May we call on you to help choose essences for other people in therapeutic situations, like massages or acutonics (sound healing)?

I would be happy to bring forth this understanding as a tool for healing in the future. We already have sound healing. This will be called sense healing.

Sandalwood has been used for clearing. In Asian cultures, when people knew that someone was going to pass away, they started burning sandalwood. Sandalwood has the capacity to clear the mind so that the soul can easily transition to the other side. Sandalwood is a gift from God. It is a smell of God.

In India, people bathe the statues of gods with sandalwood, and they place dots of sandalwood on their foreheads. This is not only to open the third eye. The third eye is between the two eyebrows, but the dot is placed a little above that. The dot is for clearing the mind and opening the angel chakra, which is right in the middle of the forehead. This is where you become aware of other realities and your connection with your guides.

If you combine sandalwood oil with a small dose of papyrus oil and add a few drops of oil of lily, you will have a good combination that can do many things, especially healing emotions stored in your cheeks. This would also support healing digestive problems in the stomach. You can apply it to the spinal column. You will feel tingling sensations and a movement of energy.

There are many smells. You can work with them and see. It is not difficult. If you think it will be difficult, it is going to be difficult. If you experiment with it, you will find a smell that supports you. That smell will be different for each of you. They are all different. But sandalwood, papyrus, and lily can support everyone, especially if you want to breathe it early in the morning when you wake up. It will give you a sense of peace in your body and your mind, along with a general sense of well-being. You will be in good spirits that day.

2. Kryon discusses some of these tales. See Lee Carroll, *The Parables of Kryon* (Carlsbad, California: Hay House Books, 2001).

After breathing that smell in the early morning, make an intention using a sound frequency. Simple sounds are enough. For example, *baam* means, "I am in the present moment." It is a strong word. It comes from the deepest part of your being. Tone it three times. You will immediately feel energy in your head. Tone this from the deepest part of your throat. You will feel sensations in your forehead or third eye, a sensation of rising light. It means: "I am fully in the moment" — not past, not future, but this moment. You will not have much worry about the future or the past. You will be in a state of joyfulness and more focused on the present.

Another oil you can try is called argan. Argan oil is made from the argan tree. It is not available in many parts of the world, but it is plentiful in some places. It is grown in Morocco. It can support healing many illnesses in the body.

• • •

Invite What You Want to Experience

This is Archangel Michael. There is a smell I would like you to experiment with: the smell of the sea in a port area. That smell can be very supportive for people who are depressed or sad.

How do we acquire the smell of the sea by a port if we need it? I live in the middle of the city, far away from the water.

Invite the sea to you. You are the Creator. Here is an experiment:

Close your eyes and visualize a dock, a port, and a ship with water gently lapping on the stones nearby. Do not go there. Invite the energy of the port to come to you where you are sitting. Just breathe it in. You will feel some sensations on your forehead. Just breathe it in. Just breathe for ten seconds.

You can open your eyes now. How do you feel?

Speaker 1: I smell it.

Speaker 2: I absolutely love it, and I smell the port in Cape Town, which is my home.

Speaker 3: I smell it, and it is visual as well.

Speaker 4: I feel this great expansion, and I can also feel the sky.

Invite what you want to experience. When you do that daily, you are truly coming into your full power as a Creator. You are in a very high level of vibration. Creation is the greatest fun you can have. Play with it, dear ones, and enjoy it. With each creation, you will feel more confident. It is fun, and you are expanding your consciousness. We are all divine magicians. This is good fun when you start doing it. You will say, "I call for the energy of the tree to come to me." This is a way of magic, so you can experience far away things just by sitting here. These are ancient teachings of magic.

Blessings, this is Archangel Michael.

• • •

Spiritual Alchemy Treats Common Ailments

Hello, my name is Och. I am the Angel of Spiritual Alchemy. Alchemy conjures up many interesting visions for people. As soon as people hear the word "alchemy," they say, "Magic! I can do magic. I can be famous. I can be 'such and such.' I can create what I want." Alchemy is truly something very different. Alchemy is the act of turning base metals into gold.

Isn't that a metaphor for changing consciousness?

It is also possible to turn base metals into gold. It has been done before. There are certain tones, sounds, and sacred geometric patterns that can bring the alchemy for change in your life in a benevolent way.

We wish to bring forth some understanding of how to use spiritual alchemy in everyday life. We are raising the energies within you and also the energies outside of you, particularly in natural kingdoms. There are many energies in nature, but they usually do not give out their secrets because they have been misused. So nature beings are very careful. In movies like *The Lord of the Rings* trilogy, you can see how nature communicates with people, like the spirit of the great tree. They will not tell their secrets because they have been misused, controlled, and manipulated.

Here is an example of using spiritual alchemy: You are having a bad day or are in a bad mood. You could bring some colors to your forehead. Imagine these colors circling around your head, starting from the forehead. These colors suck up your frustration, stress, or whatever. Wouldn't that be helpful?

We want to bring spiritual alchemy to a level for people's understanding. Let us say you have pain in your knees when you walk or when you climb stairs. By putting your hands on your kneecaps and saying certain words in an ancient language, you could feel energy and start feeling better. Spiritual alchemy on the body using sounds is possible. It has been done before. These are the kinds of alchemical energies we wish to bring forth for you to understand how to work with us and call forth our alchemical energy, anchoring it into you.

This alchemy is used to change a particular situation using sound, energy, color, and sacred geometry. If you study any spiritual alchemical process, it will always include sacred geometry. Spiritual alchemy is not for everyone. You have to build the basic steps. You can ask the permission of Archangel Michael to bring forth understanding about using alchemy in your life.

To heal your knee, place three fingers of your left hand on your left kneecap — the middle finger, the ring finger, and the pinky finger. Focus your attention there, and say the words, "Gimsah. Gimsah. Gimsah." It will bring the energy of healing angels into that part of the body.

The same would work on the right knee with the same three fingers?

Yes, you may try it now.

Yes, I am. Can you do two knees at the same time?

It is best for you to do one knee at a time. Try it out, and we will wait for you.

***Gimsah. Gimsah. Gimsah.* I can feel the energy going right to my knee. It's quite amazing.**

Do it for a minute, and you will see.

How often should a person do this and for how long?

We always say that you must do it until you feel energy moving into that part of the body and that part of the body is saturated with that energy. Only then can healing take place. If someone were to use a clock and say, "I'm going to do this for three minutes," then of course, it will not work because the intention is to please the clock, not to please the body.

Right, so do it until you feel energy.

When you feel energy moving through that part of the body, how do you feel?

I feel very lifted. This is amazing, and I'm also feeling incredibly enthusiastic about the material being revealed through this book.

Maybe humanity is ready at this time, so we are happy to bring forth this understanding.

• • •

Activate the Rainbow Code for Healing

I am Wanfa-so, the Angel of the Rainbow. Rainbows are magical. All of humanity likes rainbows, including people with hard hearts. When hard-hearted people see rainbows, something makes them soft for a while. Children enjoy rainbows. They raise their arms and flail their legs to reach rainbows. In many cultures, rainbows are seen as gifts from God.

When you see a rainbow, part of you knows it is the essence of God. There is nothing that is not God. But how can you manifest God? We work to manifest that consciousness so that everyone who sees a rainbow can feel the presence of God. Scientists have their explanations of rainbows, but we are not talking about science.

What does a rainbow evoke in you? What do you feel? Maybe love, peace, beauty, grace, or joy. We create this form and reveal the patterns of color. Have you seen an oval or circular rainbow?

Almost. I've seen double rainbows.

Oh! Yes, because we have the capacity to manifest and create on other planets and in other cultures, we can create three or four rainbows at a time.

Do you know that there is a code inside the human body called the rainbow code? You can activate the rainbow code. Then the qualities of consciousness you have when you see a rainbow can be automatically triggered within you. How about that?

Pretty good! So we call it forward to activate it?

Activate it in yourself. Interestingly, rainbow colors are the colors of the first seven chakras. But a rainbow has geometric patterns inside it. It also has mathematical codes. Do you think that it's only the colors that affect human beings? The codes of a rainbow talk to the codes and the geometric patterns inside your body on a cellular level. You do not understand why, but you feel good. Call on us, and we will guide you.

Do you know that a rainbow can also be used for healing? Many people are not aware of this. This is the essence of a rainbow. But that is just one aspect. You can use rainbow energy for healing, especially from an operation. Rainbow energy can bring faster healing to the body.

So a person simply calls forward the Angel of Rainbows. Would you be able to us about your name?

Yes, Wanfa-so means "pretty one." We are very pretty. You have to have a sense of humor. We can support humanity. In the nighttime, we can create magical patterns, and we can even make rainbows appear in the nighttime with different color patterns

What colors are the rainbows at night?

What do you think? The Aurora Borealis. Who creates them?

I know what the scientists say, but ...

That is the human mind thinking.

People see this as a very physical thing.

If a group of people calls, we can make rainbow energy appear in any part of the world. Let us say there is a problem in the Middle East, and all of you meditate and ask that rainbow energy be anchored into the ground in the place where there are great problems. There would be some relief for the people there. They would feel hope in their hearts, even considering all their problems. When humanity loses hope, then there is devastation. As long as human beings are able to be open to the light, there is possibility for change.

Could you talk a little bit more about how someone could be healed using your help and your energy?

After an operation, a person needs fast healing. We angels work inside the physical body where the operation or wound happened. These areas will start closing much faster.

Does the person need to ask for this, or can someone else ask that this be done for a person who needs healing?

Someone else can ask, but it works best when people ask for themselves. We also work with the animal kingdom. Rainbows are not just for human beings. They are for trees, birds, and all the little creatures who crawl on the ground. The energy on the planet is very heavy, and these beings are affected very much. Our help and support are very apparent to them.

Human beings are just awakening. We have been propping them up. The ancients knew about this. The Italians knew about this in ancient times. Michelangelo knew what we were doing. He even tried to paint pictures of rainbow angels. We can also influence the mind of a distraught or mentally disturbed person in order to bring some semblance of stability into the person's life.

A rainbow has higher-vibrational colors blended with the colors you see. The predominant blended color is platinum. This is directly related to the platinum ray. This is one of the highest rays, the highest energy available for humanity to work with. When you work with a rainbow, you are working directly with the platinum ray. It has a capacity to break through old belief-systems and patterns of thinking. This in turn is directly related to the eighteenth through twentieth chakras. Human beings must discover this. This is why we are coming today, to bring this understanding.

The Rainbow Pyramid Technique

On another level, you can imagine that you are sitting inside a beautiful pyramid, and there is a rainbow inside the pyramid. This could be a very powerful tool for healing. Do it right now to feel the energy.

Visualize a big rainbow and a big pyramid, and you are sitting inside the pyramid. Most people will be able to feel the energy and the expansion immediately. They will feel a calmness of mind, and their bodies will start to relax. They will let go.

How do you feel?

Relaxed and supported.

You can make a drawing of this and look at it, trusting that you are inside the pyramid. This would be very beneficial.

You can also invite rainbow energy into your bath. Fill your bathtub with the rainbow energy and bathe in it. Soak it up for thirty to forty minutes. When you finish, you will feel relaxed and not just because hot water relaxes your muscles. You will also feel refreshed inside; you will feel sacredness and purity inside as well. In that state, you can have clearer dreams, clearer visions, and clearer understanding.

We also affect the fruit kingdom, especially during summer — watermelon and other fruits. We can offer much when you call on us. Do you have any other questions, dear one?

No, but I want to thank you. This is so beautiful. Thank you for the work you do.

Blessings.

• • •

The Trial of Birth

This is Angel Mansu. The placenta is such an important connection. It connects the baby to the Divine through the mother. When the placenta is disconnected immediately after birth, the entire legacy and memory of the divine connection with the creative force is disconnected. (You may call this the feminine.) This disconnection sets up the energy of forgetfulness.

Native Americans and others in ancient times left the placenta in place for some time. When the placenta is disconnected, a vacuum is created in the child. The child feels a very deep, incredible loss, like somebody who sees a shocking death. The child experiences the tragic awareness that his or her connection with the creative force has been taken away. The baby will try to fill this vacuum. Some turn to fantasy to survive.

We, the angelic beings, support the child during this momentous time. There are angels present when the baby starts emerging from the mother's womb. As the baby takes its first breath, angels hold supportive energy. We are also there at this time, but our function has to do with the placenta and the umbilical cord. We try to ease the shock and the pain for the little one, for this is a very critical time.

Birth is much more difficult than death. An energy configuration and attunement occurs during birth. The same thing happens when someone dies. It is a doorway. But when you die, you can remember to connect with your full essence and remember more about yourself. The opposite happens in birth. In death, you bring in higher truth that will pull you upward, but in birth, it reverses and you forget.

The child remembers the comfort it had before it was born and wants to go back. It misses its family, its guides, and its support team. Although they have been prepared, they feel utterly alone. What do they do at that time? They cry out in pain. They reach out to their friends to fill this vacuum.

We support the children during this momentous time, and we are with them constantly for the first three and a half days. We support the children to acclimatize and realize that this is their new reality. They must adapt and adjust quickly. Some children become introverts right from that young age. The child's parents might be extroverts, but the child becomes completely withdrawn. These tendencies are formed at this time.

Doctors, scientists, and psychologists think a child's environment causes these tendencies. That only plays a small part. Even though we administer our love, sometimes the child does not come out of its withdrawal or fear. The child can end up growing up in the energy of withdrawal, not fully accepting his or her true qualities. Almost all humans on the Earth plane are affected by what they experience during birth to varying degrees. It is time to go back to this time and heal these wounds.

Separation from Your Soul Group

You might wonder why some children are so aggressive or violent, even from a young age. Where do they pick up this energy? You can say it is from the parents, from witnessing violence, from watching something on television, or from a past life. Yes, all of these are contributing factors, but another understanding is that it is caused by the separation they experienced during birth. What happens when something precious is taken from your life? You fight back with whatever you can, for when you lose this connection, it is a severe loss. Everyone on the planet has experienced this. It even occurs at the birth of a nation. Some nations are aggressive, violent countries.

We can heal this separation by communicating with the placenta, for it is a web. A placenta looks like a web covering the baby. In some cultures like the Japanese, sometimes the placenta and umbilical cord are kept in a box, so at least the child can have some remembrance of it if it is nearby.

We ask all of you to hold your hands on your womb and go back in time to when you were being birthed. First, there was the excitement of coming into the world, for you prepared for this. As you are born, your excitement becomes a horror because your support system is taken away.

Imagine beautiful chanting: "Ahh … moo … ooh … moo …" In the room, there is a birthing chair or a birthing bed, and you are being born. You see in your mind's eye the most beautiful loving hands, many hands, extending toward you with the greatest joy and love in their hearts. You take your first breath; a water being now becomes an air being. You become enveloped in the great love of all these hands; there are twelve pair. You are covered with the placenta, the umbilical cord, the blood, and the fluids. These beautiful gentle hands raise you to the breast of the great mother who gave you birth. The umbilical cord is not cut, and the placenta is still around you.

You hear the heartbeat of your mother, and we, the ancients, place a golden dream, like a spiral, on top of your head. Through this, we channel energies into you; and we bring them to your solar plexus, your hips, and your legs. See us fill you with this beautiful light. You are not afraid. You are not frightened. You ask to stay in this place for a moment. Now see the light from your hips going around you in a circle. This goes up to the top of your head, flows downward through your pranic tube, and down the back of your body, and it is anchored into the ground to help you ground the energy of this moment of birth. Loving hands support you. You feel the angelic presence. There is no more fear of abandonment.

One of the greatest fears humans carry is abandonment. By the time you are three-and-a-half hours old, you slowly acclimatize and realize why you were born, why you chose this way of being born, and why you chose to experience separation from your guides and support team. You slowly start to open your eyes, and your mother says, "I see a smile on the baby's face." This is the first time you fully recognize and understand you have a new family.

This was amazing. You mentioned that the Japanese keep the placenta in a box next to the baby. Does that help the baby to feel connected?

This is now done out of habit. But the true purpose when it was started was to support the baby to move through this transitioning process. The placenta is like a web around you, and then suddenly it is taken away. You immediately feel alone and disconnected. You feel you have lost the love of your mother and your entire support team, because when you are in your mother's womb, you are completely in touch with the other side. Then you are born and suddenly everything is gone. Would you not be afraid? Separation consciousness begins at birth. We support this transition period for the first three and a half days.

You know, your ancient rabbis and your ancient people knew about this. This is why birth is so significant in your culture. The elders knew and had a good understanding about the nature of reality.

Thank you. This is quite true. The mothers cook and eat the placenta and the cord during their first week with the baby. They believe the baby can connect back to the womb through the mother's milk.

That is very true. That is why I said your people understand this; very much so. This is about nurturing. When this is not done in a sacred way, often the child does not feel nurtured, and the child can grow up to be un-nurturing. People say a child's behavior is caused by what happens during their first four or five years. Of course, experiences affect the child — the energy in the house, the family, what they watch on television. But the first few days are a very critical time, for most of the basic qualities of a baby's consciousness are set then.

God Danced the Day You Were Born

If you take people through those first three and a half days after birth and connect them with love and nurturing, they can experience great healing of the emotional body. The first three and a half days set them up for the next phase of life. Between three and seven years, they form their personalities. From seven to twelve, they refine their personalities and become stronger but feel challenged; this comes from the first three and a half days. True healing must take place in that phase. Then people can heal the wounds from the rest of their lives.

This is why birth is significant in evolved societies. There is a saying in English, "God danced the day you were born." Birth is a truly significant experience. If the people around the mother sing while in joyous ceremony, the mother and the baby-to-be would set up the energy for the child to be in a beautiful environment.

In your culture and other cultures, marriage is a great celebration with singing, dancing, and joyous feelings. The groom and the bride feel supported by the people around them and by each other through their own love.

How about birth? It is a very significant event. Celebrate birth with great joy, especially just before the birth. Create joy among mothers. Call many ladies to be around the mother. You will see more and more births happening in homes and in other places, not just in hospitals. People will sing, dance, and celebrate, and the baby will feel welcomed, for even if the support system of guides is taken away, the baby will feel much love from the people around them celebrating his or her birth.

The vacuum caused by the withdrawal of guides will be suddenly filled with earthly love. The baby can feel this because babies are feeling-oriented beings.

The transition will be complete. The baby will be whole once again. The home environment will play a part, but the groundwork will have been laid with a very beautiful foundation, for these children are the adults of the future. When they are honored, when they are balanced, and when their emotions are kept in balance, they will act in a balanced way.

You can call me by my name, Mansu. It is just a simple name. I am the Angel Mansu. And when each child is born, three angels are there. Many angels support the birth process. Three of us support the placenta. Sometimes you have more than five, especially if the birth is difficult or the baby is being born in difficult circumstances.

Water Birth Supports Our Transition

Angel Mansu, I would like to know about the difference between a water birth, in which the mother is lying in water, and a regular birth like those done in hospitals.

Dear one, you are a water being. It is natural for you to be in water; you swim in water when you are in the womb. Birth is a terrifying ordeal for a baby. It comes through the birth canal, which is very narrow. Then as soon as the baby is born, it is separated from the mother, the cord is cut, the placenta is removed, and suddenly there are no guides. The baby is terrified.

We can minimize the terror as much as possible. With water births, the baby comes from the mother's womb (which contains amino acids) directly into water. At birth, the baby is becoming an air being right away. It has to open its lungs and breathe immediately; otherwise, it will die. It changes from a water being to an air being in a split second. This is why in hospitals, they often tap babies on their bottom so that their lungs open and they are able to gulp air to breathe. This is a big trauma for the babies. Just imagine that you are living in water and suddenly you are breathing air. For you, it is like being submerged in water. You become very frightened. You cannot breathe because you are used to air. It is the opposite but more terrifying for a baby. Water birth can support this transition.

In water birth, the baby moves from one water environment into another, and then slowly, in a matter of a few minutes, the baby starts breathing air. The baby is born in water, and it is not taken out right away. It is given time to adjust. Some babies even swim in the water right after they are born. There is no fear. These children will not be afraid of life. When there is no fear of life, there is no fear of death. They can become emotionally stable people. Water birth will become more and more common.

That is beautiful. I have a question as well. Would it be helpful for the people who are assisting in a birth to ask for your help by name, or do you just come automatically?

We are always there to support you, but acknowledgement can open the door much further for someone who has an understanding of the nature of angels and how we are there to support humanity. Also, we suggest that as soon as the baby is born and before you even cut the cord, you place the baby on the mother's stomach. The baby needs reassurance and to feel the heartbeat of the mother.

My dear family, this is Mansu.

CHAPTER NINE

Rejuvenate Your Physical Body

Archangel Gabriel with Goddess Roopeshwari, Archangel Michael, Archangel Metatron, Angel Lazarus, the Angels of Transition, and the Angels of Resurrection

Hello, dear friends. This is Archangel Gabriel with Goddess Roopeshwari. There is so much conflict in the world and so much fear. The dark ones are up to their old games, creating fear through conflict and control. Let all of us hold the light of God's peace.

I want to begin a very interesting discussion. Why did you choose a particular body shape? Why do humans have different shapes? There are so many different kinds of human beings. Why did you choose this color skin or this hair (or no hair) or to be short, fat, or thin?

Each shape carries out the design and the intention of what needs to be accomplished on the Earth plane. If you were to condense a human being into a sacred geometric form, what would that form be? In a manner of speaking, before you incarnate, you go to a school with a fitting room. You choose body features that will support you in what you will come to Earth to learn and master.

In your meditation, you can express the intention of going back to the fitting room at a time before you chose your body shape. This shape helped you grow to where you are now. But now you intend to re-create yourself into something entirely new, a spirit in a human body, experiencing, realizing, and accepting the new consciousness of Earth. For this new reality, you wish to have a different uniform, a different set of clothes. The technicians there will help you.

Does this mean that you will need to change bodies? Of course not, but they will change the inside of you energetically by replacing certain parts or adding new things, perhaps a shoulder pad, maybe something for the hair. This is what masters do. Have you ever seen a master with a crumpled shape or a bald head?

They all look perfect.

They look very healthy — they have beautiful piercing eyes — because they choose their bodies. You too can go back to the fitting room and choose a particular shape for yourself — different eyes, ears, or body organs. You are ready now, dear ones. This has never been revealed to the world before. We think that you are ready for these changes. You will see miracles in your life. Your overall body shape will stay the same, but you will choose your body features, your energy, and other characteristics that match the new you, the master within you. The beauty of this is that it will not take long to do this. You are evolving.

You will become a master in thirty years. You will face another reality in a new body and with a new physical appearance. You will empower yourself. Your energy will have new passion. Your eyes will be distant, like an animal's. Everyone will recognize you. This is not magic. It is a natural way. Then you can state, "My intention is to create a new body. A new energy within me will create a new reality, and my intention is to create this new reality." You will have a new name and a new body.

Who do we call forth to assist us to manifest this new body?

Ask your guides to transport you to the Creator's storage room. All the body armor is there, different types of body sets. Call on your guides to transport you there. This is Archangel Gabriel with Goddess Roopeshwari.

• • •

Putting on the Hat of a Master

I am Archangel Michael. Are there questions?

It is said that we design our screenplay before we incarnate because before we are born, we know exactly what our souls need to experience. Our body type relates to this so that we can have some experiences for the soul. What you are suggesting here could be called a new perk. We can go to the storage room and pick up a new set of threads.

Yes, exactly. Most of you have almost completed what you came here to do. Now you can open a new reality for the next phase of your life. This is why we are bringing this teaching to you. As we mentioned, we have never brought this teaching to the Earth plane. This is called putting on the hat of a master.

If you were a master, would you want to have the same physical characteristics? Perhaps you would dress differently. Maybe you would behave differently.

You could have a body that matches the new you. If you had not completed most of your lessons, you would not be here. You are here building the bridges for the next generations. This does not mean that you will not have challenges. You might still have earthly challenges because the Earth matrix is very strong, but your response to Earth challenges will be very different. They will be more solution based rather than mind based. You will want to face your challenges, resolve them, and move forward.

Is this like the magic of shape-shifting?

No. This is not like the magic of shape-shifting. Shape-shifting is done to raise your vibration by using a specific shape and then coming back to your reality. This is much bigger than that. This is the rejuvenation of your physical body.

So that we can keep the wisdom that we are gaining in this lifetime longer and to pass it on to others?

Yes, and also to have longer periods of life itself. This is what future technologies will find. In spirituality, when the student is ready, new teachers will come. It is time to extend your thinking. There is so much more you can do besides just think that something is a problem.

How does this work with DNA activation? Is that part of the renewal process?

Of course, dear one.

So it works hand in hand as we open up our DNA?

Exactly.

This is the action that activates the advanced DNA strands?

Exactly, it is huge. When you are able to take different body armor and work with it for a few days, you will see the difference right away. From that place, there is much more power within you, 30 to 100 percent more. Your work will be much more powerful, and you will be able to bilocate, go to different places, to bring healing.

When you are in this new body armor, you are much more powerful. You will hold powerful forces in you. You will not be affected by what is happening externally. You could hold all the people of Iraq or Syria in the warmth of your heart. When ascended masters walk, the radiance of their light touches thousands. When they are in a meditative state, the power they manifest is perhaps a thousand times greater. In this way, you will be able to affect many more people. You are truly becoming God within yourself.

Make an Intention Book

We are at a critical time in the world. Which way will we turn with the advent of the people who declare an Islamic nation and eliminate those who do not follow them? How can you bring light to these people? It is very difficult because they have completely suppressed their feminine aspects through fear, control, and intimidation. Only a powerful beam of light can break open the walls they have built. This powerful light comes from a master like you.

You mentioned a new shape, a new body. Can we do the same thing with our organs, or is this only for our external appearance?

When you don new armor, it is complete, not only the outer, but the inner as well. Does rejuvenation just happen on the outside? Many masters have done this.

What is the difference between a new body and the fountain of youth? Is there a connection between the two?

The fountain of youth is only a phrase used by people to help them imagine truly awakening. The true fountain of youth is awakening spiritually and then claiming and donning your new body.

What happens when you start donning your new body? It overrides and erases everything you are carrying in your physical body, including your bone structure.

• • •

This is Archangel Gabriel.

Is it correct that as your body changes, you must have the intention of being of service to others?

I would say that your intention should not only be to be of service. It is your birthright to have this new body armor so that you can bring more of your light into your being.

But is it our birthright to learn this?

Yes, exactly. On this subject, Creator gave Rae a technique, and we would like to share it with you. As you are very well aware, intention plays a very big part in the manifestation of reality. Many of you make intentions only in your minds. After two or three days, that intention is gone or you are not sending much energy into it. Do you send energy into your intentions every day? It is very important to do this.

We suggest that you get a nice notebook and a good pen. This book is your intention book, and this pen is your intention pen. When you take this pen in your hands, you know that you are going to write your highest intentions in this book.

There is a sacredness, divinity, and universal force in this action, and when you do this, you come to a very high place. Once you have written your intention, send energy into that intention for a minimum of three minutes. We ask you to keep this book because people often make intentions and after a few days, they do not even remember they have made the intention. They act differently. When you write your intention, work with it.

Are you reminding us of our own power, to take our own power back, so that we can avoid being browbeaten by our level of reality?

Exactly. We are asking you to take your power. Many masters lived alone because the energy of the spiritual matrix was very weak, but now the energy of the matrix is stronger, and you do not have to be alone. You can be in your home with your family. If you practice this for about three years, you will be able to do what you call miracles. It will become a natural part of you. There is no magic. There are no miracles. Miracles are in the natural order of things.

• • •

Laughter Is Great Medicine

This is Archangel Metatron. Humor is the medicine of the future. Even angels have humor. Laughing has been the medicine of the past, but today it is forbidden for many people. Very few people truly laugh. If you can laugh every day, making up your own story or tickling yourself, you will generate so much joy. Watch a funny video and laugh your heart out, and you will see so much tension evaporate.

When you laugh, this energy goes into the ground and the atmosphere. The world is very serious now. We need laughter to compensate. Seriousness and laughter are two sides of the same coin, like yin and yang. When you are too serious, have a good laugh. You will be able to offset that energy. When something consumes your mind and you are very serious, do something funny or think about an instance when you felt joyful, when you laughed out loud.

When you are laughing, pinch or tap yourself very lightly. You will anchor the energy of that moment in your conscious reality. Anytime you are sad, depressed, or down and out, pinch or tap your body in the same place. The experience of laughter will immediately come back into your conscious mind. This is very good for people processing difficult emotions. They can get stuck in their emotions.

You do not need to choose an episode of laughter. You can choose a happy moment in nature, making love to your partner, holding your baby's hand, or watching a beautiful sunset. When you pinch or tap yourself, you lock the energy of that moment.

• • •

Request a Resurrection Ceremony

Blessings, my friends. This is Lazarus. Is the biblical account of my experiences true? It is definitely true. What was Brother Jesus trying to show people by resurrecting me from the grave? He was exhibiting mastery. This mastery exists in every human being. Many ancient mystics have done this in India and elsewhere, including Master Sai Baba. You can ask for the energy of resurrection to be reactivated inside you. It must be called forth. You have a code called the resurrection code. It is inside every human being.

Every moment is a death moment. Each moment dies and is gone. It never returns. You are dying every moment, and your consciousness is reborn. Call forth your I Am presence, and ask to perform the resurrection ceremony. You will resurrect yourself immediately into the new you. You will see a transformation, especially now, during these special times. This time is truly a death process for many. It is a time of resurrection — the death of ideas you have held as truths, the beliefs and patterns you have carried through endless cycles of birth and death as attachments, your preconceived ideas, and (most important) the way you looked at God and creation.

Most people carry the same consciousness forward into their next lifetimes. Unless they deliberately work on themselves, very little progress is made. Because of the conditions in which humanity had to toil (in the sand, in the fields) just to survive, it was difficult to work on themselves. They did not have what you have — books, information, and wisdom from many wise teachers.

You are dying every moment, but your consciousness is not dead. You will carry the same consciousness, the same thought processes, and the same energy field for the next half-hour to hour although you died an hour ago. You are not who you were thirty minutes ago or even one minute ago. But you still carry the same consciousness or energy. This is why it is very difficult to make changes.

If you are brave enough, you can ask for this death process to receive a complete resurrection with the beloved new consciousness of your I Am presence. This was also one of the initiations performed in ancient mystery schools not once but many times. The initiations in the Great Pyramid were initiations of death and resurrection. If you are bold enough, you can ask for the initiation of death and resurrection into your new consciousness.

This is Lazarus.

• • •

Insight from the Channel

Thank you. The word "death" is scary, I must say. Is it just transition, or what exactly is the meaning of the word "death"?

From Rae: Once you activate this, you can ask for the death of your present reality and present consciousness, and then you can open up to the new consciousness. This occurred in ancient initiations. All initiations are about death and resurrection — being resurrected into something new. You might be frightened when you call for this because it can involve stripping away what you thought was your truth, things you were holding on to. You may not be able to …

To start anew.

What Lazarus said makes sense to me. For example, he said that we are dying every moment and that we never get that moment back. We are not who we were even one minute ago. Thus, we carry the same thinking process into the next moment and into the next life.

We are reborn every moment, but in the new moment, we are still carrying our old energy, thought patterns, and belief systems. When people die, they carry the same consciousnesses they had and bring them back to their next lives. Very little is achieved unless they really put conscious effort into moving forward. In former times, people were not able to do this work because they were in survival mode.

Partially it's because people were not aware that they could do this. These people are caught in a certain consciousness, which is very limiting.

I wonder whether some people want to change. Some people can get so caught up in surviving that it doesn't occur to them that other possibilities exist.

• • •

Go into Your Next Life with a Higher Consciousness

Hello, dear ones. This is Archangel Michael. We have allowed Lazarus to speak with you on this subject because there are angels for death and angels for birth. An angel can wash away everything you have carried throughout your life and replace it with a higher consciousness if you ask. If you allow him, he can rewire your thinking, your brain, or your energy structures. Angels can wash them away if you know how to call on them to receive their assistance. You can return as a blank slate, more or less, without what you have picked up in this lifetime and without what you brought from other lifetimes that is not of your true nature.

Many human beings are aware of this. Death and birth are doorways. In death, the energy that you take through the doorway determines your next life. If you believe in a loved one coming to see you, that person will manifest instantly. If you believe your master will come to see you, you will manifest it. This is the power of creation, glorified by God (millions of times) as people die.

If you are consciously dying, you can ask the Angel of Death to wash your mind so that it is clearer. This moment of utter creation can be magnificent because it comes from a place of purity. You will create this magnificence in your afterlife, and your next life will have this higher consciousness. Teach the people this. Call on the Angel of Death. It will give people comfort to know that there are angels supporting their transitions and clearing away their minds just before death happens. They will be able to go in peace, not carrying all their garbage. "Garbage" is a strong word, but this can help them a lot.

For example, in Israel two nations (both brothers) fight each other, ready to kill and maim each other. What happens when one brother is killed? He carries the hatred of what the other did to him. It works both ways. They are buried in the ground, and this affects the energy of Mother Earth's body. Then they come back with the same energy. So the cycle of hatred continues. This is why there has been very little peace in that part of the world, because there is so much hatred in the hearts of both nations.

Angels can wash away this hatred before a person exits his or her body. That person would no longer carry hatred. The body would become as a soothing balm for Mother Earth because it would no longer carry the dense energy of hatred. People would be reborn without hatred.

Angels Can Replace Your Cells' Consciousness

Many children now being born are called Crystal or Indigo children. They have a higher frequency because they do not carry past memories. For them, the past and who did what do not matter. They say, "Let us start fresh from now." They are in a completely new state. There is no fear, only glorious creation. Their minds are affected by the past, and they draw from the past what they want to create. They are concerned about the future. If their past is very clear, then their present will be clear as well.

You can call for this angel and have a death process ceremony or initiation. Call for the resurrection angels and be reborn again. Are you ready to do this? It can transform you. This is a high level of initiation. You do not have to use the word "death" if it scares you. This is a transition from one reality to another reality within the same physical body.

Do you call them transition angels?

Yes. You can call the Transition Angels and also the Resurrection Angels. We bring this new tool to humanity. Imagine in your everyday life that the past did not matter. "He said 'this.' She said 'that.' Your wife said 'something else.'" Without that, you are in a joyful place. Most conflict is caused by the past. Most hatred comes from the past.

Everybody carries something from the past. Sometimes you see a strange person and feel strange. Something is triggered from the past — a memory, an experience, an energy — so you react.

The past affects you a lot, much more than you realize. When you call the transition angels to clear away your mind, transition happens; then call resurrection angels to resurrect you in a new consciousness. They work with your cellular structures. Your bones are your wisdom keepers.

There are angels who work in your body to replace the consciousness carried in your cells. Your cells will naturally do what they are designed to do; they resurrect. Bring forth this deep-seated consciousness that is already there. Right now it is deeply buried in all your dense thoughts and all the dense food you eat. Cells have to work very hard to digest this food. There is no time to look at their original intention, which is God consciousness. We encourage you to work with these two groups of angels, the transition angels and the resurrection angels.

• • •

Release the Energy of War from Land and People

Hello, my dear friends. We are the Transition Angels. We work with the resurrection angels.

You [Fredaricka] live in a land where great atrocities have taken place since before the time of King Herod and continue to this day. The remnants of that energy still exist. You can go to places where the children killed by Herod are buried and call forth the transition angels to release the many souls that are still stuck on the Earth plane. They are very attached, and they do not realize that they have died. Call for the resurrection angels, and request the children be reborn with a new consciousness. You will do a great service to many souls.

Your country has been invaded many times. When killed instantly in battle, many do not realize that they have died, and they can carry this consciousness for eons of time. Ask for the souls who are ready to move on, and call the angels to work with them. This will benefit the land, benefit the souls, and of course, benefit you.

The same thing is true for the Americas. A great genocide took place; Many millions of Native Americans were killed. This is very rarely talked about, and this is why you see so much hatred and violence in that country. People who like to do earth healing can work with these angels, because those souls affect the present reality in more ways than you can imagine. They affect your reality through the energy of thought processes. When your vibration is low, you are easily influenced by these energies. Add this to the energies being downloaded to Earth by the forces that want to control people. So these people are affected twice.

Work with these angels, release the souls, and bring peace to them and peace to the land. Then ask that the resurrection angels work with these souls, resurrecting them with a clean state of mind and consciousness. What you do on an individual basis can be accomplished for a nation.

Resurrection angels are very powerful. They change your body structure and your vibration. They help you manifest a new body template. Body templates can be damaged when someone dies by physical injury or other means. Work with the resurrection angels. They can repair a damaged body template. We are not talking about natural aging or repairs to a natural body. This is important work and must be done. Otherwise, the beings who are born can carry defective auras. Their etheric bodies are already damaged, and the physical body must be rectified. Resurrection angels can do that.

I [Fredaricka] certainly would love to assist these children. During that time, they were searching for Master Jesus. There are certainly a lot of little babies and children who were murdered here in Israel. I will do my best to give assistance.

This is very important work; the land can be healed, and these souls can be released, for they can be trapped for eons. It is only a wise soul who can help them by calling on the angels to support their transitions. These souls will be reborn in a new state of consciousness without the hatred from the past. That happens when you work with the resurrection angels. They repair the consciousness and the memories inside the cellular structure. This is where true healing takes place. When the cellular structure is healed, the souls are reborn with a more intact aura field, and they become centered and clear.

The resurrection angels play a very vital role. Almost all the ascended masters who worked on this planet have worked with us continuously. You must continuously call for this frame of resurrection within you.

What is ascension? Is it not a transformation? Is it not a resurrection? Something old in you dies and becomes something new through alchemical transformation. The resurrection angels are part of the ascension process of humanity.

There is so much hatred in the world. People are killed and suffer from the crises in the Middle East and other places. What happens when these people transition? They return with the same consciousness of hatred, revenge, and unforgiveness. The cycle continues. Call on the resurrection angels not only for you but also for Earth and the ground that stores these energies.

America is fighting a battle of revenge. Americans feel attacked, so they retaliate regardless of the collateral damage. Americans now live in fear in a completely controlled society. Imagine how the resurrection angels could heal this revenge. Then life would be very different. Follow the same method to heal individually and collectively for the country. Call on these angels to work with you.

Work with these angels in your life and in your community. When you bring healing to others, you are healed and uplifted. You will gain more than you put out through the laws of interaction. We are the Angels of Resurrection and the Angels of Transition.

• • •

Transition Angels Alleviate the Fear of Death

Most people are afraid of dying. Teach them about transition angels and resurrection angels. Then you will have taught them well, and a lot of their fear of dying will go away. Most people fear what they will experience when they die. If they know there are angels waiting to support them just by calling on them in this most important time of their lives, then their fear can be changed to peace.

Can you give us some guidance about how often to work with these angels? Suppose we are trying to heal our countries. How often would this be done? Would it be done more effectively with a group of people?

You can start with your own community with a group of people. It requires tremendous power to heal a country.

With a few people?

Or by yourself in your Berkshires. All people who transitioned are still on the Earth plane. How can you help them?

We were talking the other night about how the Native Americans were expelled from this area in the early nineteenth century and the misery this caused, so that would be a good place to start.

Right now, a great settlement has been reached for one of the communities in America.[1] The American government has finally admitted its mistake and has given a large settlement to a Native American [Navajo] community. This is one step. Of course, you also need to bring the energy of the healing.

Would it be appropriate for us to be very specific? We live near a place called Stockbridge, and the Stockbridge Indians were part of a great exodus from this area to Wisconsin. Should we get that specific, or should we just ask to be facilitators for the angels' work?

All is possible, whatever you feel. Yes, this exodus caused them great sorrow. You can work in your neighborhood in your own way; call on the specific area or a larger area. Healing must happen to the land, and working with angels can bring much faster healing.

How often should we do this? Once a month? I'm not trying to be too specific here, but once is probably not enough. Is that correct?

---

1. Sari Horwitz, *Washington Post*, "U.S. to pay Navajo Nation $554 million in largest settlement with single Indian tribe," September 24, 2014, accessed February 17, 2015, http://www.washingtonpost.com/world/national-security/us-to-pay-navajo-nation-554-million-in-largest-settlement-with-single-indian-tribe/2014/09/24/4dc02cc6-434e-11e4-9a15-137aa0153527_story.html.

I would say to help an individual, one time is enough, but for a collective — for a nation or a larger area — you need to do it until you feel it is time to move on and that you have done the work. For an individual, one time is okay. You will sense a shift; you will feel it in your heart. You will feel a difference in your consciousness. You will feel a sense of lightness coming into you. You will sense more peace and more clarity coming into you.

The other night in an energy healing session, a woman that we knew when we were children was very present. She had been murdered thirty years ago. I didn't know about calling the angels forth then, but I did speak with her because she was in the room with us. She did get some peace. But this is an example of what you are talking about, is that correct? She came forth, and now we can ask the angels to help her. Is that how it should be done?

Exactly, if she is ready to move on, she will not carry the energy of hatred or sorrow about what happened with her. She will go with a much clearer, peaceful mind, and that will become part of her new reality. She will no longer carry the hatred of what happened to her, so she will not have to come back for retribution.

This seems like a very powerful tool to help Earth heal.

Of course, very true.

• • •

Experience the Power of the Resurrection Prayer

You are so much more than your thoughts. Your physical body is getting older, but your mind is always getting sharper. If you think you are getting old, you will experience what old people experience, and that will become your reality. If you believe your body is aging in a perfectly healthy manner and your mind is sharp, that will become your reality.

We ask you to do the resurrection prayer every day:

I resurrect my mind.
I resurrect my health.
I resurrect my finances.
I resurrect my creativity.
I resurrect joyful creation in my life.
I resurrect peace in my life.
I resurrect holy communication.

Work every day to cleanse and purify, and after that, let this resurrection prayer be a part of your life. I am the light. Through this prayer, you will see miracles happen. If you have problems with your leg, say, "I resurrect my leg to be in perfect health." If you have problems with your eyes, say, "I resurrect my eyes to be in perfect health." Jesus showed this. His life was an example, and he said, "Truly, truly, I say to you, he who believes in Me, the works that I do, he will do also" [John 14:12, NASB]. For example, you can say, "I resurrect peace in Israel once again."

Resurrect everything that is broken in your life. Everything in your life that is broken can be fixed and repaired. Say, "I am the resurrection. I am the light."

This is Archangel Metatron.

• • •

Hello, dear family. This is Archangel Michael. This prayer can truly change your life and any situation or condition. I ask you to hold this prayer in your heart and repeat it many times until it becomes a part of you:

> *I resurrect my life. I resurrect my healing. I resurrect my capacity to love, to attract, and to be with a loving and benevolent partner.*

You will see a gradual easing of tensions, steady growth. It will be an expansive time, so hold this prayer in your thoughts every day.

CHAPTER TEN

You Are the New Masters

Creator

Blessings to all. Scriptures have said that when the student is ready, the teacher appears. You are an advanced level of students, and we are able to bring forth new understanding to the world.

There will be many more who want to come to speak and to participate in creating a new reality. In past times, an avatar would appear, like Buddha, Jesus, Sai Baba, or Kabir. Many brought understandings on a mass level. Now we will see teaching coming through beings who have worked on themselves. They bring forth their truth not like the old masters who sat alone and meditated for long periods but new masters who walk among the people.

This is the beauty of this time. Imagine a benevolent being coming from a benevolent planet and landing in front of you. What would you do? Many beings would throw themselves at the being's feet because the being would be glowing with light. They would think this is the Creator. No.

Now you will have teachers who are everyday people: a manager at a cabaret club, a waiter at a restaurant, a football coach. They will be the new teachers — ordinary people and masters. But who will know they are masters?

There is always new wisdom available on the planet if you seek it. It is the seeking that draws the wisdom forth. When you seek, there is a heat wave coming from you. You will seek to find where what you are looking for is available, and it will be brought forth to you.

The Beginning of an Era

The year 2015 (the year of 8) is a marvelous year. The heat-seeking missile from your heart can travel far distances and bring forth understanding. This year of 8 is a year of completion for many and the beginning of a new era.

Throughout most of the planet, you will see the beginning stages of a reset. People will say collectively, "This is not what we wanted. There is something drastically wrong. Let's try to change things." Individually, people will say, "It is time for a reset, time to change my belief systems. This supported me, but it does not support me any longer. I am going to do things differently."

When something comes up in your life, you could say it is coming up for release so that a new beginning can happen. The year 2015 is significant in terms of rebirth. This will pick up speed by the time March arrives, and after the solstice in March, it will move much faster. Do not be afraid of this year, for it will bring to the surface what needs to be cleared. Not only that, it will also plant fresh seeds for a new beginning.

Death and rebirth happen at the same time. Some of you will feel it. You will say, "Something died, but I am still alive. I am going to start something new." Welcome this. Embrace this. Everything is in position, in divine order.

This is Creator.

About Rae Chandran

Rae Chandran was born in India and has lived in the United States and Japan. He performs individual channeling sessions for his clients, and he has published articles in the *Sedona Journal of Emergence!* Rae teaches workshops throughout the Far East on the Ancient Egyptian mysteries, DNA activation, and channeling. He creates soul symbols for his clients, and he leads tours of ancient holy places worldwide.

Rae founded the Omran Institute, which promotes DNA awareness and certifies practitioners of Omran 12-Strand DNA Activation. He also performs individual Omran 12-Strand DNA sessions for clients. Rae lives with his wife and children outside of Tokyo, Japan. Visit his website at www.RaeChandran.com.

About Robert Mason Pollock

Robert Mason Pollock was born in Washington, DC, and has lived in London (England), Canada, and the Berkshire mountains of Massachusetts. He is an energy healer at a holistic health resort in the Berkshires, and he has an energy healing practice with locations in New York City and the Berkshires.

Robert wrote *Navigating by Heart*. He teaches workshops in spirituality and DNA activation. He also performs individual Omran 12-Strand DNA sessions for clients. Robert currently lives in the Berkshires, and his website is www.BerkshireEnergyHealing.com.

Rae Chandran

$19.95 • Softcover • 384 PP. • ISBN: 978-1-62233-013-3

32 color pages of mudras and images to activate your 12 levels of DNA

DNA of the Spirit, vol. 1

Channeled through Rae Chandran

with Robert Mason Pollock

The etheric strands of your DNA are the information library of your soul. They contain the complete history of you, lifetime after lifetime; a record of the attitudes, karma, and emotional predispositions you brought into this lifetime; and a blueprint, or lesson plan, for your self-improvement. Your DNA is also a record of your existence from the moment of your creation as a starbeing to your present incarnation. This information is written in every cell of your body.

CHAPTERS INCLUDE:

- Mudras for Activating the Twelve Layers of DNA
- The Awakening of Crystalline Consciousness
- Auspicious Times for Awakening Consciousness
- Angelic Support for DNA Activation
- The History of Human DNA
- Your Internal Compass: Nature's Body Intelligence

Rae Chandran

$16.95 • Softcover • 192 PP. • 978-1-62233-027-0

DNA of the Spirit, vol. 2

Channeled through Rae Chandran

with Robert Mason Pollock

This companion book to *DNA of the Spirit, Vol. 1* originated with the intention and desire to bring forth understanding to support humanity. Go through this volume while holding a sacredness inside of you, asking that the material be imprinted in your sacredness so that it may become an experience that you will be able to live.

Some of the material in this book is coded, and sincere students will find they can open these codes. Understanding can be received through your own filter and in your own way. This way, you will find the Divine within.

CHAPTERS INCLUDE:

- Auric Imprinting Technique for Healing
- The Number of God
- Reveal Your Life Contracts
- Re-create Your Life with Your Akashic Records
- Humans Are Creators in Training
- Use Shape-Shifting for Regeneration
- How to Activate the Codes Within You
- From Darkness unto Light: the Aquarian Age
- Discover Your Energy Connections to Beings of Light
- Understand the Sacred Geometry of the Human Body
- Determine What Drives Your Soul

Light Technology PUBLISHING

Tom T. Moore

AVAILABLE IN SPANISH

THE GENTLE WAY

A SELF-HELP GUIDE FOR THOSE WHO BELIEVE IN ANGELS

This book is for all faiths and beliefs with the only requirement being a basic belief in angels. It will put you back in touch with your guardian angel or strengthen and expand the connection that you may already have. How can I promise these benefits? Because I have been using these concepts for over ten years and I can report these successes from direct knowledge and experience. But this is a self-help guide, so that means it requires your active participation.

$14.95 • 160 PP., SOFTCOVER • ISBN 978-1-891824-60-9

EL CAMINO AMABLE

$14.95 • 176 PP., SOFTCOVER • ISBN 978-1-62233-260-1

THE GENTLE WAY II

BENEVOLENT OUTCOMES: THE STORY CONTINUES

You'll be amazed at how easy it is to be in touch with guardian angels and how much assistance you can receive simply by asking. This inspirational self-help book, written for all faiths and beliefs, will explain how there is a more benevolent world that we can access and how we can achieve this.

These very unique and incredibly simple techniques assist you in manifesting your goals easily and effortlessly for the first time. It works quickly, sometimes with immediate results — no affirmations, written intentions, or changes in behavior are needed. You don't even have to believe in it for it to work!

$16.95 • 320 PP., SOFTCOVER • ISBN 978-1-891824-80-7

THE GENTLE WAY III

MASTER YOUR LIFE

Almost three years have passed since *The Gentle Way II* was published. Yet as many success stories as that book contained, I have continued to receive truly unique stories from people all over the world requesting most benevolent outcomes and asking for benevolent prayers for their families, friends, other people, and other beings. It just proves that there are no limits to this modality, which is becoming a gentle movement as people discover how much better their lives are with these simple yet powerful requests.

$16.95 • 352 PP., SOFTCOVER • ISBN 978-1-62233-005-8

FIRST CONTACT

CONVERSATIONS WITH AN ET

$15.95 • 224 PP., SOFTCOVER • ISBN 978-1-62233-004-1

COMING SOON

ATLANTIS & LEMURIA

THE LOST CONTINENTS REVEALED

Light Technology PUBLISHING Presents

by Cheryl Gaer Barlow

Angels Explain Death and Prayer

"We are the angels of the Mallbon. We are meant to tell those of Earth that the death of the body is never to be feared. We help in ways not understood by humanity. We can manifest anything we desire. We can live as humans on Earth. When we absorb the reality of Earth, we work God's wonders in ordinary ways.

"When the surroundings are not in focus or when you feel unable to cope with the people or circumstances around you, be still and ask God for help. God will respond to requests of help by mending emotions with aid from the angels. This is done by being aware of the angels. We surround you and bring you comfort.

"You must, as a human race, lift the quality of thought to the highest level. When the level of thought is low and miserable, it is generated through the entire world. When it is lifted to a level of joy, it lifts all minds. When you know the teachings of the angels, no ignorance will be left in the soul. You will no longer be afraid or in pain. Now is the time to stand with the angels of God and help humankind."

—The Angels of the Mallbon

$16.95 Plus Shipping

ISBN 13: 978-1-62233-008-9
Softcover • 224 PP.
6 X 9 Perfect Bound

Angels Explain God and the New Spirituality

$16.95 Plus Shipping

ISBN 978-1-62233-023-2
Softcover 176 PP.
6 X 9 Perfect Bound

"The message of this book is to tell the souls of Earth about the wonders of God, the glorious angels, the heavens, the Earth, and all existence. Know above all things that God loves you more than any words can express.

"God is always with you. He is ever bringing you toward the blossoming of your soul. God communicates by way of the holy angels of God. The most important words we want to tell you are these: Open your soul. Surrender your soul to God. Ask God to lead you to truth, love, and peacefulness. Ask God for any attributes you wish to acquire. God's angels will help you become the strong, powerful soul that you are meant to become.

"A world of souls, lifting their minds to reach God will affect the universe. Be the soul you are meant to be. The most powerful attribute a soul may attain is love."

—The Angels of the Mallbon

Light Technology PUBLISHING Presents

BY DRUNVALO MELCHIZEDEK

LIVING IN THE HEART

Includes a CD with Heart Meditation

"Long ago we humans used a form of communication and sensing that did not involve the brain in any way; rather, it came from a sacred place within our hearts. What good would it do to find this place again in a world where the greatest religion is science and the logic of the mind? Don't I know this world where emotions and feelings are second-class citizens? Yes, I do. But my teachers have asked me to remind you who you really are. You are more than a human being — much more. For within your heart is a place, a sacred place, where the world can literally be remade through conscious cocreation. If you give me permission, I will show you what has been shown to me."

— Drunvalo Melchizedek

\$25.00 Softcover, 144 PP.
ISBN 978-1-891824-43-2

Chapters Include:

- Beginning with the Mind
- Seeing in the Darkness
- Learning from Indigenous Tribes
- The Sacred Space of the Heart
- The Unity of Heaven and Earth
- Leaving the Mind and Entering the Heart
- The Sacred Space of the Heart Meditation
- The Mer-Ka-Ba and the Sacred Space of the Heart
- Conscious Cocreation from the Heart Connected to the Mind

Drunvalo Melchizedek's life experience reads like an encyclopedia of breakthroughs in human endeavor. He studied physics and art at the University of California at Berkeley, but he feels that his most important education came after college. In the past twenty-five years, he has studied wizh over seventy teachers from all belief systems and religious understandings. For some time now, he has been bringing his vision to the world through the Flower of Life program and the Mer-Ka-Ba meditation. This teaching encompasses every area of human understanding, explores the development of humankind from ancient civilizations to the present time, and offers clarity regarding the world's state of consciousness and what is needed for a smooth and easy transition into the twenty-first century.

Phone: 928-526-1345 or 1-800-450-0985 • Fax: 928-714-1132

Light Technology PUBLISHING Presents

THE ANCIENT SECRET OF THE FLOWER OF LIFE, VOLUME 1

Once, all life in the universe knew the Flower of Life as the creation pattern, the geometrical design leading us into and out of physical existence. Then from a very high state of consciousness, we fell into darkness, the secret hidden for thousands of years, encoded in the cells of all life.

Now, we are rising from the darkness, and a new dawn is streaming through the windows of perception. This book is one of those windows. Drunvalo Melchizedek presents in text and graphics the Flower of Life workshop, illuminating the mysteries of how we came to be.

Sacred geometry is the form beneath our being and points to a divine order in our reality. We can follow that order from the invisible atom to the infinite stars, finding ourselves at each step. The information here is one path, but between the lines and drawings lie the feminine gems of intuitive understanding.

You may see them sparkle around some of these provocative ideas:

- Remembering our ancient past
- The secret of the Flower unfolds
- The darker side of our present/past
- The geometries of the human body
- The significance of shape and structure

$25.00 Softcover, 240 PP.

ISBN 978-1-891824-17-3

Drunvalo Melchizedek's life experience reads like an encyclopedia of breakthroughs in human endeavor. He studied physics and art at the University of California at Berkeley, but he feels that his most important education came after college. In the past twenty-five years, he has studied with over seventy teachers from all belief systems and religious understandings. For some time now, he has been bringing his vision to the world through the Flower of Life program and the Mer-Ka-Ba meditation. This teaching encompasses every area of human understanding, explores the development of humankind from ancient civilizations to the present time, and offers clarity regarding the world's state of consciousness and what is needed for a smooth and easy transition into the twenty-first century.

Tina Louise Spalding

Jesus: My Autobiography

This insightful book is designed to free you from the limitations of your conditioned mind and to give you a better understanding of Jesus's life and teachings so that you can begin to transform your mind, your heart, and the world. Through Tina Louise Spalding, Jesus tells his story in his own words, clearing up misconceptions and untruths and describing his physical and nonphysical journeys that led to enlightenment.

$16.95 • Softcover • 256 pp. • ISBN 978-1-62233-030-0

Great Minds Speak to You

"Many in spirit look on these times of difficulty, abundance, trouble, and innovation and wish to share with you their experiences and ideas. Some famous names and faces will come to mind as you read this book, and you will glean some fine information about their own learning, their own suffering, and indeed their own experience in the life after this life, for they all wish to tell you that there is no death as you perceive it to be. They are all there in their astral forms, enjoying their continued growth, their continued expansion, and their continued joy in living."

— Ananda

$19.95 • Softcover • 192 pp. • ISBN 978-1-62233-010-2

CD of Live Channelings Included!

Making Love to GOD
The Path to Divine Sex

"We are here to teach the way to divine bliss, and we know you are scared — scared to lie naked caressing your lover with rapt attention and honor. Give love all day, and you will be guaranteed to receive love all night. The divine sexual experience connects you, God, and your lover — if you have one — together in a dance of divine bliss."

— Ananda

$19.95 • Softcover • 416 pp. • ISBN 978-1-62233-009-6

HILARY JAMRON

We all have reasons for doing the things we do.

We all have our own realities. It is my blessing to have more than one.

— Hilary Jamron

$16.95 • Softcover • 304 PP.
978-1-62233-014-0

Surrealistic TRIALS

When Hilary died, part of her soul refused to come back. That part of her higher self chose to remain where peace and simplicity reign. From that time forward, life would reveal itself in front of her, and she would simply step into her future. Decisions would be made without fear or hesitation by an unconscious multidimensional consensus, and she would survive. She would travel through death and paralysis without self-pity or delay.

The truth is that each of us is as limitless as space and time, having no boundaries, beginnings, or endings. Limits are illusions, delusions, like pebbles that we casually kick out of our way as we move forward. Illness, pain, heartbreak, and life circumstances are all pebbles. There's no point in looking back when we've already kicked our earthly problems off to the side of the road. The kicking is a gentle toss of the foot done in perfect synchronicity to the drumbeat of lessons learned. After that, the only direction is forward.

Light Technology PUBLISHING

Sarah Goddard Neves

12 Steps to a Lightness of Being

This unique book has been designed as if you were taking a very special spiritual development course in the comfort of your own home. Through its wisdom and guided meditations — **included on the enclosed CDs to boost empowerment** — *12 Steps to a Lightness of Being* will gradually but surely lift your vibration and awaken you. Therefore, to get the most out of it, decide now not to rush it but to read it slowly. Take as long as you need on each step before moving on to the next. Commit to doing each meditation or visualization, giving yourself some quiet, undisturbed time to do this, and recall your meditation experiences and insights afterward. By doing so, you will get the most out of reading this book.

3 GUIDED MEDITATION CDs INCLUDED!

$19.95 • Softcover • 160 pp.
6 X 9 • Perfect Bound
ISBN 978-1-891824-99-9

The Twelve Steps:

1. Meditation on the Light
2. Opening to Your Intuition
3. Master Connection
4. Being Happy
5. The Healing Power of Forgiveness
6. Evolving with Love and Light
7. Realizing Your Life's Purpose
8. Awakening to Love
9. You: a Creation and a Creator
10. Soul Reflection
11. Hope from the Stars
12. Becoming a Lightness of Being

Shifting Frequencies

Sounds for Vibratory Activation

with CD

by Jonathan Goldman

For the first time, Healing Sounds pioneer Jonathan Goldman tells us about shifting frequencies — how to use sound and other modalities to change vibrational patterns for both personal and planetary healing and transformation. Through his consciousness connection to Shamael, angel of sound, Jonathan shares his extraordinary scientific and spiritual knowledge and insights, providing information, instructions, and techniques on using sound, light, color, visualization, and sacred geometry to experience shifting frequencies. The material in this book is both timely and vital for health and spiritual evolution.

$17.95 Plus Shipping

ISBN 978-1-891824-70-8
Softcover • 226 PP.
6 X 9 Perfect Bound

CHAPTERS INCLUDE:

- Sound Currents: Frequency and Intent
- Vibratory Resonance
- Vocalization, Visualization, and a Tonal Language
- The Harmonics of Sound
- Vocal Harmonics and Listening
- Energy Fields
- Creating Sacred Space

Hearing the Angels Sing:

A True Story of Angelic Assistance

by Peter Sterling

Hearing the Angel's Sing chronicles my extraordinary journeys into the higher dimensions of light where I met the angels who ultimately brought me to the realization that my mission was to be a channel for God's heavenly music. The book includes never-before-shared details of my journey of awakening. From the snowcapped peaks of the Rocky Mountains to the tropical jungles of the Mayan temple lands, the red rock towers of Sedona, and ultimately to the Incan highlands of Peru, this is a captivating story that will take you on an amazing journey of discovery!

— Peter Sterling

$16.95 Plus Shipping

ISBN 13: 978-1-891824-96-8
Softcover • 256 PP.
6 X 9 Perfect Bound

CHAPTERS INCLUDE:

- Descension and Birth
- Down the Rabbit Hole
- Windows to Heaven
- Rocky Mountain High
- Angels and Devils
- Harmonic Converging
- Red Rocks Calling
- To Hear the Angels Sing
- Fires of Purification